PI-YAHHHHH!!
The Cajun Ninja's Cookbook

JASON DEROUEN

83
PRESS

PI-YAHHHHH!!
The Cajun Ninja's Cookbook

83 Press
2323 2nd Avenue North
Birmingham, AL 35203
83press.com

ISBN: 978-0-9794090-8-0
Printed in China

CONTENTS

DEDICATION

I dedicate this book to anyone who has ever taken the time to watch, comment, like, or follow The Cajun Ninja Facebook and YouTube pages. There's so much that goes into the process, so whether you're a close friend, family, or we've never even met, it's truly an honor to have your support.

I also proudly dedicate this book to my wife, Misty—Mrs. Cajun Ninja. I couldn't have made it this far without her. The amount of time that she has sacrificed so there would be a quiet kitchen for me to film in is unfathomable. I'm truly grateful for her. She is the greatest gift the good Lord has ever brought to me, and it's been wonderful sharing this journey with her.

Jason

INTRODUCTION

Ladies and gentlemen, we finally did it: The Cajun Ninja cookbook. If you are a longtime supporter, you know exactly what this means. So many of you have asked for this. Right after going viral in 2016, the two main questions were, "Where can I get that pot?" and "Do you have a cookbook?" LOL. I'm sorry I held off for so long, but to be quite honest, I wanted this to be something very special. Throughout this book, you'll see many highlights of all the important things in my life. This book is something sentimental that my children will be able to pass on to their own children one day. So, grab a spoon and your favorite beverage; it's time to get your pot HEATED UP!

It may come as a surprise to learn that becoming a popular online cook wasn't a goal in my life. Don't get me wrong; I've always loved to eat, but when I was a kid growing up in Houma, Louisiana, I was much more interested in martial arts and making people laugh than I was in mastering a roux.

My mom is a registered nurse and worked a lot of night shifts when I was a kid, but when she cooked, it was a real treat. Every year for my birthday, she would cook whatever I wanted. (She still does this to this day!) More often than not, I remember asking for smothered pork chops. I vividly remember how tender the pork chops were and how the gravy soaked into the rice. You can find my version of my best memory of those pork chops in this book. My dad wasn't much of a cook, but he had a huge passion for cooking shows. He would watch Emeril Lagasse on television almost every night. Occasionally, I would be right alongside him, taking in every "Bam!" along the way. Looking back, this was probably where I first discovered the entertainment side of food.

I was 23 when I first decided to try my hand at cooking. I didn't even know the basics. At the time, I was a lead singer in a local cover band and had absolutely no intention of a cooking career. But, our lives are full of surprises. You never really know where your path is going until you take that next step. I remember researching all my favorite Cajun dishes on the internet. Early on, I would even call my mom to get her feedback on some of my favorites. Of course, being the Cajun mom she is, she'd usually just offer to make it herself and bring it over. If there's anyone who loves to cook for others, it's definitely her. For anyone who has a Cajun mom: if ya know, ya kneaux.

Through many years of trial and error, cooking became simpler for me. Soon, I was making gumbo, jambalaya, and étouffée and boiling crawfish on the weekends. But it wasn't so much the cooking that I loved; it was entertaining others. In May of 2016, I decided to start a Facebook page geared toward entertainment. I posted random, entertaining bits and pieces, but never anything cooking-related. As a matter of fact, doing cooking videos was the furthest thing from my mind. But in the fall of 2016, some cool weather came through, and I decided to cook a gumbo. I had a wild hair to Snapchat the process. Then I put all the clips into a video and uploaded it to the Facebook page I created. Little did I know, this video would change my life forever.

In the video, I threw the trinity into the pot yelling my first "Pi-YAHHHHH!!" I should mention, because of my father, my love for martial arts is deeply ingrained in me. I'm a fourth degree black belt in Taekwondo and run a school in Houma called Home of Martial Arts. I also take Jiu-Jitsu lessons from

Sensei Scotty Smith at Next Generation in Thibodaux. So, yelling something like "Pi-YAHHHHH!!" was nothing out of the ordinary for me. I remember hearing it many times growing up. My grandmother lived in Raceland, Louisiana, and many of my uncles would pick with me, being I was a young martial artist.

Around the time of uploading the gumbo video, the page had about 400 followers. More than half of those followers were my friends and family. Within a couple of days of the gumbo video going live, the follower count skyrocketed to about 15,000. Within two days, the video hit more than 1 million views. The rush of comments and messages was very overwhelming. I can assure you, though, the feedback wasn't all positive. Many Southerners have strong opinions about gumbo, and my version drew much criticism. Not-so-fun fact: the negativity really got to me, and I almost deleted the page. Before coming to that conclusion, I decided cooking is an interpretation of your own preferences. We're often drawn to dishes and methods that remind us of how our grandparents, parents, aunts, and uncles cooked, so it's only natural that we're opinionated. To this day, I'm so glad I overcame the negativity. The following week, after the gumbo video went viral, I decided to continue posting cooking videos.

In my second cooking video, I did my first chopping of the onions with my hand (something you'll see in almost all my videos now). After a loud "Pi-YAHHHHH!!," I said, "Don't mess with The Cajun Ninja!" Subconsciously, this was a nod to my Cajun heritage and my love of martial arts. Soon, people began calling me that, and I officially became known as "The Cajun Ninja." As more and more people began to try my recipes, the love and support started to grow. Currently, my Facebook page has more than 1 million followers. I couldn't be more grateful for all the support.

At the heart of all this is my family. I'm not The Cajun Ninja without being a dad and a husband. My family is everything to me, and I couldn't do this without them, especially my wife, Misty. I often say she is the backbone to all of this. She has even adopted the name "Mrs. Cajun Ninja" on social media. I love that she did this; it proves how supportive she is of this endeavor.

When I first decided to type "Pi-YAHHHHH!!," I chose the number of H's to represent each person in my home—my wife, my three daughters, and myself. I put two exclamation points in case we ever had a fourth. I figured it kind of looked like an H and it would have been a big surprise to us since we stopped at three kids. Now, I like to add that the two exclamation points represent our dogs Gumbo and Hazel. The H's themselves stand for healthy, happy, humble, heartfelt, and home. I always want this to be the foundation for what goes on under my family's roof. No amount of popularity should change this.

So, you'd think I'm all set, right? Well, lo and behold, my girls hit me hard about getting a baby golden retriever. How's a man supposed to say no to his loving wife and beautiful baby girls? So, I told them, "Well, what can we name him? Everything in Pi-YAHHHHH!! has been taken, the only thing left is a dash." We now have a golden retriever named Dash. I can't say I ever anticipated this, but he's awesome, and I'm so pumped that this book captures his debut.

I'm immensely thankful for all of you who have followed my journey. You all are the true celebrities. Without your support, The Cajun Ninja would only be a blank page. So, please, with the utmost sincerity, enjoy every recipe and feel free to make any necessary adjustments. Remember, no matter what anyone tells you, when it comes to cooking, "You Deux You." ("You do you" with Cajun flare.)

DEROUEN DICTIONARY

PI-YAHHHHH!!: Fancy way Cajuns mix "pow" and "hi-yah." Anything that smacks is "Pi-YAHHHHH!!" whether it's good food or a conk on da head. LOL.

YOU DEUX YOU: Don't be afraid to try things you think you may like. It's actually "You Do You" but with a little Cajun flare. *Deux* is French for "two," which makes even more sense to me, because you shouldn't give a crap what anyone thinks when it comes to cooking for yourself. I want people to hone in on their own preferences, because we all have our own unique palate. You get the one life; discover yourself by doing what works for you. You deux you!

LET'S GET CRACKALACKIN': A saying that's been thrown around for as long as I can remember. I started using it early on in my cooking videos as my way of saying let's get this show on the road.

TRUSSME: Trust me. When it comes to Cajun cooking, I'll never lead you astray. You can trussme on that.

THE HOLY TRINITY: The "holy trinity" in Cajun cooking is the starting base for many Louisiana favorites. It is a vegetable medley that consists of chopped onions, bell peppers, and celery. For Cajun favorites such as crawfish étouffée, gumbo, and jambalaya, you'll start by sautéing the holy trinity.

THE POPE: Just like people call chopped onions, bell peppers, and celery the holy trinity, they refer to garlic as the pope.

GET YOUR POT HEATED UP!: It's time to get down to business. Crank up that heat and let's get started.

FIXIN'S: The extra stuff. Sometimes it's the corn, sausage, mushrooms, and so on that I cook with boiled crawfish, and other times, "fixin's" refers to the toppings for a bowl of chili or a roast beef po' boy.

CAJUN KITCHEN ESSENTIALS

- Large Dutch oven
- 100-quart pot for boiling crawfish
- Boiling bags
- Flat-edge wooden spatula
- Peanut oil
- Pi-YAHHHHH!! Seasoning
- Liquid crab boil
- Seafood boil seasoning
- Hot sauce
- Long-grain rice
- Chicken stock
- Seafood stock
- Dried red beans
- Smoked sausage
- Tasso
- Crawfish tails
- Shrimp
- Crabmeat
- Corn
- Red potatoes
- Yellow onions
- Green onions
- Bell peppers
- Celery
- Garlic
- Dried bay leaves
- Salt
- Cayenne pepper
- French bread
- All-purpose flour
- Butter
- Purple, gold, and green sanding sugars

THE CAJUN NINJA'S SPICE OF LIFE

In December of 2020, I launched Pi-YAHHHHH!! Seasoning. It was a recipe I'd been working on for a couple years. I knew I wanted to come out with a seasoning that had less salt and more kick. I wanted something that, if you ate it raw, it would pop you in the mouth, but if you cooked with it, it would balance well. There was so much trial and error in getting this right. I had to measure out the grams of every ingredient. It was like Breaking Bad (the AMC drama series) of seasoning in my kitchen. Nevertheless, I'm happy with the overall result of the seasoning. I understand it may not be for everyone, and I'm OK with that. I always want people to choose what's best for them. However, if you like a li'l kick in ya life, give it a try.

1 | *BACK TO BASICS*
GROUND RULES OF CAJUN COOKING

CRAWFISH BOIL

MAKES 10 TO 20 SERVINGS

8   lemons, halved
6   navel oranges, halved
1   cup orange juice
1   (63-ounce) container seafood boil seasoning
2   cups salt
½   cup liquid crab boil
1   (35- to 45-pound) sack live crawfish
6   small yellow onions, quartered
6   heads garlic, halved
1   bunch celery, cut into 4-inch pieces
1   pound carrots, peeled and cut into 4-inch pieces
2   pounds smoked sausage, cut into 4-inch pieces
3   pounds small red potatoes, halved
1   pound whole button mushrooms
1   (8-ounce) container Spicy Cajun Seasoning
12 to 24 frozen half ears corn

Optional Items:
Boiling bag for fixin's
Asparagus, cauliflower, Brussels sprouts
Frozen tamales
Boudin
Cayenne pepper

1. In a 100-quart pot, fill to the halfway mark with water. Turn burner on high.

2. With basket in pot of water, squeeze in all lemons and oranges. Add orange juice. When the water looks like it's at a slight boil, add seafood boil seasoning, salt, and crab boil. Stir, cover, and bring to a rolling boil.

3. Meanwhile, rinse crawfish by dumping them into an ice chest, spraying them, and letting water drain. Keep doing this until the water looks clear.

4. Once pot is boiling, place onions, garlic, celery, carrots, sausage, potatoes, and mushrooms into boiling bag, and drop into pot. Cover and let boil for

20 minutes. For other fresh items, such as asparagus, cauliflower, and Brussels sprouts, you're going to want to add those to the bag with about 8 minutes left. When the 20 minutes is up, remove bag to a tray; set aside. Let drain, and then dump fixin's into a couple other trays. This will make you a great host, as your guests can munch on this while the crawfish cook.

5. Next, remove the basket from the pot, and discard lemons and oranges. Set aside basket, and add Spicy Cajun Seasoning to the pot. (You do this because all the fixin's have soaked up much of the initial seasonings. If you like even more kick, add cayenne pepper.) Make sure the pot is still at a good boil. Add crawfish to basket, and slowly place into pot, and cover. Boil for 3½ minutes from the moment you drop in the basket and cover. Once the time is up, turn the burner off and let the crawfish soak for 37 minutes.

6. At this time, if you have frozen tamales, be sure to individually wrap them in foil, slightly clamping the ends. With about 30 minutes of soaking left, add frozen corn, frozen tamales, and boudin. Doing it this way will cook the frozen items to a great consistency. Furthermore, the temperature will drop, which will prevent the crawfish from overcooking yet still allow them to soak up the seasoning. Be sure to stir the bottom to the top every 10 minutes.

7. When the time is up, pull the basket up from the pot. Hold for a moment as remaining liquid drains back into the pot. Once you see barely anything draining from the basket, dump crawfish into a clean ice chest. Be sure to have something that slightly props open the ice chest so it doesn't completely close. You don't want them to overcook in there.

8. Have a large scooping shovel and serving trays available so people can serve themselves a desired amount. Enjoy!

BLACK BELT TIP

A general rule of thumb is to cook 3 to 5 pounds of crawfish per person, but with all of the fixin's that I cook with mine, this recipe can feed 10 to 20 people.

TALES FROM THE BAYOU

Spring is an exciting time in Louisiana thanks, in part, to crawfish season. There's not much that I love more than boiled crawfish. Misty and I like to invite family and friends over on the weekends and do a big crawfish boil. I'll pick up a few sacks at West Main Seafood in Thibodaux, and we'll spend the day in our backyard cooking, talking, and eating crawfish with our favorite people.

BOILED SHRIMP

MAKES 8 TO 10 SERVINGS

2   gallons water
1   cup orange juice
3   lemons, halved
2   oranges, halved
¾   cup seafood boil seasoning
¼   cup salt
2   tablespoons liquid crab boil
3   yellow onions, halved
3   pounds small red potatoes
2   pounds smoked sausage, cut into 3-inch
     pieces
1   head garlic
1   pound whole button mushrooms
8 to 12 frozen ears corn, cut into 4-inch
     pieces
4 to 5 pounds large fresh shrimp
¼   cup Pi-YAHHHHH!! Seasoning

1. In a large stockpot over a high heat, bring 2 gallons water to a boil. Add the orange juice. Squeeze in lemons and oranges, dropping them into the pot afterward. Add the seafood boil seasoning, salt, and liquid crab boil to water. Mix well. As it starts to come to a boil, remove the lemons and oranges. Add the onions, potatoes, sausage, garlic, and mushrooms. If you have a mesh boiling bag, you can use this, but it helps if you have a pot with a built-in strainer. Cover and boil on a high heat for 20 to 25 minutes. (Monitor heat so it doesn't boil over.) After the allotted time is up, transfer all fixin's from the pot to a tray; set aside.

2. Add frozen corn to the pot, and return to a boil. As soon as it reaches a rolling boil, cook corn for 3 minutes. Turn heat off. Add shrimp and Pi-YAHHHHH!! Seasoning, and stir. Let it sit for 5 to 8 minutes, depending on the size of your shrimp, stirring periodically. After the allotted time, remove the shrimp from the pot, let cool for a few minutes, serve, and enjoy!

BLACK BELT TIP

You always want to use shell-on shrimp for this, but whether you use head-on or head-off shrimp is up to you. If you want a dip to serve this with, make my Seafood Dip on page 34.

My mom was my first real inspiration when it came to home-cooked meals. She was the cook of the house. One of her favorite things to do now is to sit down with a tray of boiled seafood and an ice-cold beer and reminisce over good times.

GUMBO ROUX

MAKES 10 TO 12 SERVINGS

⅔ cup cooking oil (vegetable, canola, or peanut)

1 cup all-purpose flour

1. Heat a large pot over a medium-low heat for about 5 minutes. Add oil and then flour. Begin stirring right away, pressing the flat end of a wooden spatula against the bottom of the pot. This will prevent any of the roux from sticking to the pot. Continue slowly stirring for roughly 1½ hours. It could even take up to 2 hours, depending on how low the heat is. You will gradually see the roux color go from tan to peanut butter to caramel to chocolate.

The darker the roux, the more depth of flavor you will have to your dish.

2. When you've reached the desired color, you can move forward with your recipe and add your vegetables. If you are saving it for a later day, turn off the heat, and let cool for 1 hour.

3. Once cool, much of the oil will rise to the top. You can carefully drain and discard the excess oil. From there, scoop the roux into an airtight container. The roux can last for up to 6 months in the refrigerator or up to a year in the freezer.

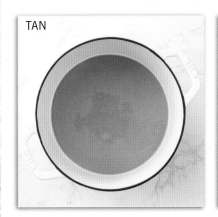

TAN

PEANUT BUTTER

CARAMEL

BLACK BELT TIP

This amount of roux is good for roughly a gallon of liquid or less. If you use more liquid, you'll need more roux. I like to use a wooden or bamboo spatula with a flat end, like my Pi-YAHHHHH!! spatula, to stir the roux. The flat edge scrapes across the bottom of the pot keeping the roux from sticking.

FRIED FISH

MAKES 6 SERVINGS

2 to 3 pounds fish fillets
1   gallon cooking oil (see Black Belt Tips)
2   tablespoons hot sauce
2   tablespoons yellow mustard
2   cups all-purpose flour
2   large eggs, lightly beaten
2   cups yellow cornmeal
3   tablespoons Pi-YAHHHHH!! Seasoning
½   tablespoon garlic powder
½   tablespoon salt

1. Start out by patting the fish fillets dry with some paper towels.

2. Afterward, in a large pot, begin slowly heating up the cooking oil over a medium heat to roughly 400°.

3. In a small bowl, mix hot sauce and mustard. Using a basting brush, coat both sides of fish with hot sauce mixture. Batter all sides of the fish with the flour. Shake off any excess. Using a basting brush, coat both sides of the fish with the egg.

4. In a large container, mix the cornmeal, Pi-YAHHHHH!! Seasoning, garlic powder, and salt.

5. At this point, check the temperature of your oil, and make sure it's at or around 400°. If it has gotten higher than 400°, just lower your heat until you reach that mark.

6. You want to quickly batter the fish with the cornmeal mixture, shaking off any excess, and then fry. The quicker you go from batter to fry, the better the crispiness of the fish will be after frying.

7. Fry the fish for 3 to 4 minutes or until golden and crispy. Layer the fish over some dry paper towels, and let cool for a few minutes. Enjoy!

BLACK BELT TIPS

Catfish, bass, speckled trout, sacalait, redfish—these are just a few of my favorite kinds of fish to fry up using this recipe.

Whenever you're frying stuff, you want to make sure your cooking oil has a smoke point higher than 425°. I prefer peanut oil, but you can also use sunflower oil.

TALES FROM THE BAYOU

We seem to live a very technology-driven fast-paced life these days. Nonetheless, it is important for me to show my girls the true luxuries of life: enjoying the outdoors, seeing the world, and even just a simple fishing trip down Bayou Black. There's nothing like catching fish. The thrill of seeing your cork go underwater is simply incredible. I can literally sit there all day and just keep casting. I thoroughly enjoy knowing that anything can happen on each cast. Here, my Juliet and Zoey were excited to show Mom some perch they caught. Although these were a little small to fry up, we had some stock in the freezer that we pulled out and fried up that evening.

FRIED SHRIMP

MAKES 4 SERVINGS

1 gallon cooking oil (see Black Belt Tips on page 26)
2 pounds large fresh shrimp, peeled and deveined
2 tablespoons yellow mustard
2 tablespoons hot sauce
2 large eggs
2 cups all-purpose flour
2 tablespoons Pi-YAHHHHH!! Seasoning
½ tablespoon salt, plus more to taste
½ tablespoon garlic powder

1. In a large pot, heat oil over a medium-low heat until it registers 425° on a deep-fry thermometer.

2. Meanwhile, in a large bowl, combine shrimp, mustard, and hot sauce. Mix thoroughly, and refrigerate for about 30 minutes.

3. When oil reaches 425°, turn heat to low. Maintain until ready to fry.

4. With about 10 minutes left on the shrimp, whisk the eggs, and add to the shrimp mixture.

5. In a small bowl, mix together flour, Pi-YAHHHHH!! Seasoning, salt, and garlic powder.

6. When you know your oil is around 425° and you are ready to fry, that is when you mix your shrimp in with your flour mixture. Add a few shrimp at a time to the flour mixture, allowing some excess marinade to drip off. Immediately after battering shrimp, place them in hot oil. Quickness is optimal for a nice, crispy texture.

7. Fry shrimp for 2 minutes and then remove. Let the excess oil drip and then place shrimp on a plate layered with paper towels. Season with a little bit of salt if you like, but it's completely optional. Let them cool a bit, and enjoy!

BLACK BELT TIP

Serve with some fries and your favorite dipping sauce or pile the shrimp onto a bun to make a po' boy. If ya know, ya kneaux!

FRIED OYSTERS

MAKES 4 SERVINGS

1 gallon cooking oil (see Black Belt Tips on page 26)
1 large egg
2 tablespoons hot sauce
2 tablespoons yellow mustard
2 pounds freshly shucked oysters (see Black Belt Tip)
1 cup all-purpose flour
1 cup plain yellow cornmeal
2 tablespoons Pi-YAHHHHH!! Seasoning, plus more to taste
½ tablespoon salt, plus more to taste
½ tablespoon garlic powder
Lemon wedges and tartar sauce, to serve

1. In a large pot, heat oil over a medium heat. You'll eventually want to reach 425°. Monitor the heat every so often with a thermometer, making sure it's not heating too quickly.

2. While the oil is heating up, whisk together egg, hot sauce, and mustard. Pour over oysters. Mix thoroughly, and refrigerate for about 30 minutes.

3. As you're getting closer to the 425°, mix the flour, cornmeal, Pi-YAHHHHH!! Seasoning, salt, and garlic powder.

4. When the oil is around 425° and you are ready to fry, pull a few oysters at a time from the bowl so the excess marinade can drip off. Add the oysters to the flour mixture, and mix well so they coat evenly. You quickly want to go from battering the oysters to frying them. Quickness is optimal for a nice, crispy texture.

5. Fry the oysters for 2 minutes. Remove the oysters with a spider strainer, letting the excess oil drip, and then place the oysters on a pan that's layered with paper towels. Season with a little bit of salt or Pi-YAHHHHH!! Seasoning if you like, but it's completely optional. Let them cool a bit, serve with lemon wedges and tartar sauce, and enjoy!

BLACK BELT TIP

If you have a container of oysters that are in liquid, pour the oysters into a strainer so that the excess liquid can drain.

TALES FROM THE BAYOU

Louisianans are blessed to have access to some of the best seafood in the country. From shrimp and crab to many varieties of fish and oysters, there's no question why seafood is a part of so many of my favorite Cajun meals. Gulf oysters are known to be big and meaty but with a mild, delicate taste. They're hard to beat, especially when they're breaded and fried like these.

PERFECT RICE ON THE STOVE

MAKES 6 SERVINGS

2 **cups long-grain rice**
4 **cups water**
Salt, to taste

1. Pour rice in a medium pot, and add 4 cups water. Bring to a boil on a high heat. Add desired amount of salt for flavor. When your water starts to boil, cover the pot, and lower the heat to a simmer. Simmer for 25 minutes.

2. After 25 minutes is up, remove from heat, and let sit for 5 minutes before uncovering. Fluff rice with a flat-edge spoon, serve, and enjoy.

BLACK BELT TIP
Every 1 cup of uncooked rice will require 2 cups of water. Some prefer to wash their rice a few times before adding to the pot. This is completely optional. Washing rice will clean some of the starch from the rice. It's up to you.

TALES FROM THE BAYOU
What's there to say about an ingredient that is so essential to a region's cuisine? Acadian settlers brought rice to Louisiana from the Carolinas hundreds of years ago and folks discovered that the warm, humid climate and all the bodies of water here were perfect for growing rice. Now, we're the third-largest rice-producing state in the whole country, and it's a part of tons of Cajun meals. If you didn't know that, you're about to find out with all of the dishes in this book. Whether it's stuffed with rice, served over rice, or rice is the main ingredient, we Cajuns can't get enough.

SEAFOOD DIP

MAKES 1½ CUPS

1 cup mayonnaise
⅓ cup ketchup
½ tablespoon garlic powder
½ tablespoon ground black pepper
1 teaspoon chili powder
1 teaspoon Worcestershire sauce
½ teaspoon smoked paprika
¼ teaspoon salt
¼ teaspoon cayenne pepper

BLACK BELT TIP

From boiled and fried seafood to my Boudin Balls (page 82) and Fried Chicken Tenders (page 81), this dip is good served with many dishes.

1. Combine all the ingredients together and enjoy! Store in an airtight container in the fridge to save leftovers for a few weeks.

TALES FROM THE BAYOU

This here is my pops, Leroy. He had a major influence on my martial arts career. Honestly, if it wasn't for him, I don't know if I would have gotten into martial arts. Every time a new Van Damme movie came out, we were always first in line to rent it. He loves getting together for crawfish boils. Besides the ice-cold Bud Light in my beer fridge, his favorite thing is my Seafood Dip. He will literally clean out the bowl with his finger.

HOMEMADE CHICKEN STOCK

MAKES 20 CUPS

5   quarts water
1   yellow onion, quartered
2   stalks celery, cut into 3-inch pieces
3   carrots, peeled and cut into 3-inch pieces
1   bunch green onions, cut into 3-inch pieces
2   (3- to 4-pound) whole chickens
2   tablespoons salt
1   tablespoon garlic powder

1. Heat up a large stockpot filled with 5 quarts of water over a high heat.

2. Add the yellow onion, celery, carrots, and green onion to the stockpot. Add the chickens. As the water starts to reach a slight boil, you will start to see some foam come to the top. Take a large spoon, skim the foam, and discard. Once you have gotten much of the foam removed, add the salt and garlic powder. Once you've reached a complete boil, cover, lower to a simmer, and let cook for 1 hour.

3. Remove the chickens from the pot. You'll want to let them cool for at least 1 hour before you begin removing the chicken from the bone. Feel free to save the chicken for another day, or continue on making whatever desired dish you like.

4. Strain the stock through a fine-mesh sieve. If you want, you can eat the remaining veggies as a snack. At this point, your stock is done; you can either let it cool and freeze it, or move forward with any dish where chicken stock is needed. Enjoy!

BLACK BELT TIP

Now listen here: you can always use store-bought stock in my recipes. Don't let anybody tell you differently. But when you have the time to make your own stock, it really does add great depth of flavor to dishes. This recipe makes a lot, but you can always freeze leftovers. Just let the stock cool slightly, about 30 minutes, and pour it into a freezer-safe container, making sure to leave 1 inch of headspace since the stock will expand as it freezes. A good space-saving tip is to pour the stock into a gallon-size resealable plastic freezer bag. Seal it and lay it flat in the freezer.

HOMEMADE SHRIMP STOCK

MAKES 20 CUPS

5   quarts water
2   pounds head-on large fresh shrimp
1   yellow onion, quartered
2   stalks celery, cut into 3-inch pieces
3   carrots, peeled and cut into 3-inch pieces
1   bunch green onions, cut into 3-inch pieces
2   tablespoons salt
1   tablespoon garlic powder

1. Heat up a large stockpot filled with 5 quarts of water over a high heat.

2. Peel the 2 pounds of shrimp. Save the heads and peelings. You can vacuum-seal the shrimp, and freeze for up to 6 months.

3. Add the yellow onion, celery, carrots, and green onion to the stockpot. Add the shrimp peelings, salt, and garlic powder. Once you've reached a complete boil, cover, lower to a simmer, and let cook for 1 hour.

4. Strain the stock through a fine-mesh sieve. If you want, you can eat the remaining veggies as a snack. At this point, your stock is done; you can either let it cool and freeze it, or move forward with any dish where a shrimp or seafood stock is needed. Enjoy!

BLACK BELT TIP

If you have leftovers, don't worry. Just freeze it for later. Find my tips for freezing stock on page 37.

Thanh Le is a professional mixed martial artist and longtime friend of mine. He is a fifth degree black belt in Taekwondo who has reached the highest levels in MMA by winning the ONE FC Featherweight Championship. He started out by competing at the very same south Louisiana TKD tournaments I myself competed in as a kid. He has great love and respect for his family and the state of Louisiana, and I'm honored to call him a friend.

Spring in Louisiana means crawfish.

2 | BAYOU BREAKFASTS
MORNING MEALS THAT HIT

TALES FROM THE BAYOU

As a young ninja, one of my favorite things my mom would make was her egg rolls. The recipe was something she had learned from my aunt Dawn but perfected in her own way. These things were so good that no egg roll was ever the same for me thereafter.

In my early days of cooking, I knew I wanted to learn how to make them. As with most Cajun moms, it was tough to get the recipe out of her. It was always, "I do a little bit of this and a little bit of that." Now, listen, I was lucky to even get that. These things were always a huge hit, so she held on to this recipe very tight. Nonetheless, I was able to get enough out of her to eventually put my own twist on them.

Just like Mom's, mine also became a hit with my guests.

One morning, Misty said she was craving egg rolls, I then said, "You know, the egg rolls call for breakfast sausage, ground beef, and cabbage. I betcha I could sub that ground beef and cabbage for scrambled eggs and bacon and make breakfast egg rolls." My wife's eyes lit up.

That night, I began working on them. I knew I would need to do the filling the night before to give me a little time so that they would be ready for breakfast in the morning. The finished product resulted in my wife pretty much hurting herself eating them. To be honest, some have even said they prefer them over the regular egg rolls. So, break out the eggs and let's get crackalackin'!

BREAKFAST EGG ROLLS

MAKES ABOUT 42

1 pound maplewood- or applewood-smoked bacon
Vegetable oil, as needed
1 yellow onion, chopped
3 stalks celery, chopped
1 bunch green onions, chopped
1 pound breakfast sausage (hot blend preferably)
½ tablespoon Pi-YAHHHHH!! Seasoning
12 large eggs
½ cup whole milk
½ stick salted butter
1 (8-ounce) block sharp Cheddar cheese, shredded
2 (16-ounce) packages egg roll wraps

1. Preheat your oven to 350°.

2. Heat up a large pot over a medium heat.

3. Place your bacon strips on a large baking sheet.

4. Bake for 15 to 20 minutes, monitoring regularly. You're going to want to take the bacon out just before reaching crispy. It's OK if you think you're taking it out too early. You just don't want them to be too crispy, or you'll end up with hard pieces of bacon in the egg rolls.

5. While your bacon is cooking, drop a small amount of oil in the hot pot, coating the bottom. Add the yellow onion, celery, and green onion, and sauté for 10 minutes. Add the breakfast sausage and Pi-YAHHHHH!! Seasoning. Cook until the sausage is browned and crumbly. When the onions start to look translucent, set the heat to a low setting, and stir regularly.

6. Cut the bacon into small strips. (The bacon will be hot, so be careful or just wait until it cools a little bit.)

7. Add the bacon to the sausage mixture. Cook over a low heat for another 5 minutes. Turn the heat off, pour the mixture into a sieve to let any excess fat drip over a plate of paper towels. Put the mixture in a large bowl, and let cool in the refrigerator overnight. Now, if you want to do this in one day, put the bowl in the freezer for 1 hour. Make sure you put the bowl on some type of oven mitt or towel. Don't put a hot bowl on a glass shelf.

8. After the filling has cooled for the allotted time, take it out of the fridge or freezer. It's going to look like it hardened or congealed, but this is OK. The next process will help shape everything.

9. Heat a large nonstick skillet over a low heat for few minutes.

10. In a large bowl, whisk together the eggs and milk. (You will not have to season the eggs. With the bacon, cheese, breakfast sausage, and Pi-YAHHHHH!! Seasoning, there will be plenty of flavor.)

11. Add the butter to the hot skillet. Once the butter has completely melted, add the egg mixture to the skillet. Let the eggs sit until the edges start to look cooked. Gently start folding the eggs until they are scrambled and done. Add the hot eggs to the filling, and stir. This will break up the filling and cool the eggs. Add the cheese, and mix.

12. At this point, add about ½ inch of vegetable oil to a frying pan. Set to a medium-high heat and just let that heat up to roughly 350°. You don't want too much oil, because if the egg rolls are able to float, they will be hard to flip.

13. At this time, prep the baking sheet you plan to put your finished egg rolls on by layering with paper towels.

14. Fill a bowl halfway with water.

15. Time to wrap. Sometimes it's safe to save one wrap to test the oil. It's a personal preference on how much stuffing you put per egg roll. I usually do roughly 2 full tablespoons. Follow the directions on how to wrap them according to the package and use the water and a basting brush around the edges so you can seal the egg rolls.

16. When you are done wrapping, drop the egg rolls, one at a time, into the frying pan. When you start to see some browning forming on the sides, flip them. Monitor each egg roll from there by flipping. When they start to look golden, remove and set on the baking sheet layered with paper towels. Let them cool for a few minutes, and you're good to go! Enjoy.

BREAKFAST CASSEROLE

MAKES 8 SERVINGS

1 pound bacon
1 (30-ounce) package frozen mini hash brown potatoes
Salt and ground black pepper, to taste
1 tablespoon vegetable oil
1 pound hot blend breakfast sausage
1 Vidalia onion, chopped
1 red bell pepper, chopped
1 green bell pepper, chopped
1 tablespoon minced garlic
6 large eggs
½ pint heavy whipping cream
½ tablespoon Pi-YAHHHHH!! Seasoning
1 cup shredded Cheddar cheese (fresh is best)
Garnish: chopped fresh parsley

1. Preheat the oven to 350°.

2. Lay the bacon and frozen hash browns out on separate large baking sheets. Season the hash browns with salt and black pepper just to give them a little flavor.

3. Heat a large pan over a medium-low heat. Add oil to coat the bottom. Add the sausage, and cook until browned and crumbly. Remove the sausage from the pan, and place in a bowl off to the side.

4. Meanwhile, if the oven has reached 350°, place the bacon on the top rack and frozen hash browns on the middle rack.

5. Bake for 30 to 40 minutes or until both bacon and hash browns are crispy. You may want to flip the bacon midway through the cooking process.

6. Add the onion and bell peppers to the pan that the sausage was cooked in. Cook down over a medium-low heat for roughly 20 minutes. Add the garlic, and cook down for another 5 minutes. Add the sausage back to the pan, and turn the heat off.

7. When the bacon and hash browns are done, remove from the oven, but leave the oven on. Make sure the bacon has sat out over some paper towels so that any excess grease has drained off. Chop the bacon into small pieces, and set aside.

8. In a large bowl, whisk together the eggs, cream, and Pi-YAHHHHH!! Seasoning.

9. Spray a 13x9-inch baking dish with cooking spray. Spread the hash browns in the baking dish. Add the vegetables and ground sausage over the hash browns. Pour the egg mixture evenly throughout the dish. Sprinkle the cheese and bacon over the top.

10. Bake for 30 to 40 minutes or until you see some browning forming on the cheese. Let cool for about 5 minutes. Sprinkle with chopped parsley, if desired. Serve and enjoy!

PI-YAHHHHH!! SCRAMBLED EGGS

MAKES 2 SERVINGS

6   **large eggs**
2   **tablespoons whole milk**
½   **teaspoon Pi-YAHHHHH!! Seasoning**
1   **tablespoon salted butter**

1. Heat a nonstick pan over a low heat for about 5 minutes.

2. In a medium bowl, whisk the eggs, milk, and Pi-YAHHHHH!! Seasoning.

3. Add the butter to the pan, and move the pan around so the butter covers the bottom completely. Add the egg mixture to the pan. Let the eggs just sit. As you start to see the edges cook and the whites of the eggs coming through the bottom, slowly fold over the edges of the eggs to center. You want to fold the eggs over so they start to stack. Remove the pan from the heat, let sit, and fold the eggs over again. Repeat this until the eggs look like they're starting to cook but still runny. Bring the pan back to the heat for just a bit if they seem very runny. Continue folding over and then remove from heat. This will slow down the process so you can get your eggs to your desired doneness. When all egg looks fluffy but still moist, they're done. Enjoy!

My wife, Misty, LOVES bacon! If I'm making scrambled eggs, there better be a big plate of bacon to go with it.

BLACK BELT TIP

The key to perfect scrambled eggs is a little Pi-YAHHHHH!! Seasoning and a little time. Don't rush the process by cranking up the heat; have patience and cook them low and slow for the best results.

FRENCH TOAST

MAKES 5 SERVINGS

7 large eggs
½ cup whole milk
½ teaspoon salt
½ teaspoon vanilla extract
2 tablespoons granulated sugar
1 tablespoon firmly packed light brown sugar
½ tablespoon ground cinnamon
¼ teaspoon ground nutmeg
10 slices Texas toast
1 stick salted butter
Maple syrup and confectioners' sugar, to serve

1. Start out by heating a large skillet over a medium heat.

2. In a large bowl, whisk up the eggs, milk, salt, and vanilla extract very thoroughly.

3. In a small bowl, mix the granulated sugar, brown sugar, cinnamon, and nutmeg.

4. Dip each slice of bread, front and back, in the egg mixture and place on a baking sheet.

5. Sprinkle your desired amount of sugar mixture on each side of the bread. Be sure to gently handle the bread when flipping over to sprinkle the other side.

6. Use the end side of the stick of butter to melt some of the butter in each spot on the pan. Place individual slices of bread in each spot on the pan where you have melted butter. Sear both sides of the bread until they are a golden brown. Serve with some maple syrup and a sprinkle of confectioners' sugar. Enjoy.

TALES FROM THE BAYOU

This is Lieutenant Percy Mosley. When I was 17, still in high school, I was a young bus boy working at Copeland's. Late for work one day, I decided to pass a car on a bridge over a bayou to catch a green light. As I got close to the light, I saw Lieutenant Mosley up ahead. He pulled me over. After some questioning, he informed me that he could cite me for passing in a no passing zone, reckless operation of a vehicle, and driving without a driver's license. (I had forgotten my wallet at home that day.) He ended up letting me go so I could make it to work. He later told me it was my mentality that led to him letting me go. I stayed polite and owned up to my mistakes. I'm grateful for that lesson, and forever apply it to my life.

HOMEMADE BUTTERMILK BISCUITS

MAKES ABOUT 12

2	sticks cold salted butter
2½	cups compacted self-rising flour
1	tablespoon granulated sugar
1	tablespoon baking powder
½	teaspoon baking soda
½	teaspoon salt
1½	cups whole buttermilk
½	stick salted butter, melted

1. Refrigerate the 2 sticks of cold butter overnight, or place in the freezer for 30 minutes to 1 hour.

2. Preheat the oven to 425°. Line a baking sheet with parchment paper.

3. In the bowl of a stand mixer fitted with the paddle attachment, beat the flour, sugar, baking powder, salt, and baking soda on a low setting, letting the dry ingredients blend for about 2 minutes.

4. Shred the 2 sticks of frozen butter with a cheese grater, and gradually mix it in with the dry ingredients. Place in the freezer for about 30 minutes.

5. At this point, if you have a dough kneading attachment for your mixer, change out the mixing attachment for the dough kneading attachment.

6. Turn the mixer on a low setting. Gradually add in the buttermilk. Continue kneading the dough for 5 to 6 minutes. During this process, you may need to turn off the mixer and use a flat utensil to help mix in some to the flour. Once the dough is pulling clean from the sides and all dry ingredients seem to be mixed in, turn off the mixer.

7. Sprinkle some flour over a clean surface. The dough will be damp, so scoop the dough out with the flat utensil onto the floured surface. Sprinkle some flour over your hands and the top of the dough. Flip the dough a few times so the outer parts of the dough are covered in flour.

8. Roll the dough to about 1 inch in thickness. Fold the dough in half two times and then roll out again to 1 inch in thickness. Fold the dough again two times and then roll out to 1 inch in thickness.

9. Use a 2½-inch biscuit cutter to cut out roughly 9 biscuits. At this point, you may be able to reshape the remaining dough and cut out another 3 biscuits. Place on prepared baking sheet. Brush the melted butter over the biscuits using a basting brush.

10. Bake on the center rack for 15 to 20 minutes or until some slight browning starts to form on top of the biscuits. Let cool for a few minutes. Serve and enjoy!

BLACK BELT TIP

I eat these biscuits fresh out of the oven with butter, strawberry jam, and a big cup of coffee to drink.

CINNAMON ROLLS

MAKES 12

Dough:
½ cup lukewarm water
¼ cup plus 1 tablespoon granulated sugar, divided
1 (0.25-ounce) package rapid-rise instant yeast
1 stick salted butter
3 cups all-purpose flour
2 teaspoons baking powder
1 teaspoon baking soda
½ teaspoon salt
½ cup whole milk
1 large egg

Filling:
1 stick salted butter
⅓ cup granulated sugar
⅓ cup firmly packed light brown sugar
1½ tablespoons ground cinnamon

Icing:
2 cups confectioners' sugar
¼ cup whole milk
2 tablespoons salted butter, melted
1 teaspoon salt
1 teaspoon vanilla extract

1. For dough: Start out by mixing the ½ cup lukewarm water, 1 tablespoon granulated sugar, and yeast in a small bowl. Let sit for roughly 10 minutes.

2. Melt the stick of butter in the microwave for 20 to 30 seconds, and set aside.

3. In the bowl of a stand mixer fitted with the paddle attachment, beat the flour, baking powder, baking soda, salt, and remaining ¼ cup granulated sugar at low speed for about 2 minutes.

4. For this next part, it's best you have the dough kneading attachment for your mixer. Switch to the dough kneading attachment. Add the yeast mixture, melted butter, milk, and egg. Beat at medium speed until all dry ingredients are blended in and the dough is pulling away from the bowl. You may have to turn the mixer off at times and move things around just so all dry ingredients blend evenly. When the dough is smooth and pulling away from the bowl, turn the mixer off.

5. Spray a large bowl with cooking spray.

6. Form the dough into a ball, and place in the bowl. Cover the bowl with a damp towel, and let sit out for 2 hours. The dough will have risen. Punch the dough down, and cover with a damp towel again. If planning to cook the next day, refrigerate overnight. If not, let proof for 1 hour more.

7. The next day, remove the dough from the refrigerator, and let sit out for 1 hour so it can come back to room temperature.

8. For filling: As you're getting close to that 1-hour mark, melt the butter for about 30 seconds in the microwave, and set aside.

9. Mix the sugars and cinnamon in a bowl.

10. Preheat the oven to 325°.

11. Sprinkle some flour over a clean countertop.

12. Punch down the dough again. Remove the dough from the bowl, flatten out a bit with your hands, and place both sides of the dough down on the sprinkled flour. This will help prevent the dough from sticking when rolling out. Roll out roughly a 20x11-inch rectangle. The melted butter should be cool enough by now so you can evenly spread it over the dough. Spread with a basting brush. Sprinkle the sugar mixture over the melted butter.

13. Spray a 13x9-inch baking dish with cooking spray.

14. Take the long end of the dough and gently fold over three or four times, or until you have a log. Taking a sharp knife, slice the log into 12 rolls. Add each individual roll to the baking dish so you have 3 rows of 4.

15. Bake for 30 to 40 minutes. Let stand for about 5 minutes.

16. For icing: In a medium bowl, mix the confectioners' sugar, milk, melted butter, salt, and vanilla extract. Make sure all ingredients are well blended. Add as much of the icing as you would like to the cinnamon rolls. Serve and enjoy!

BLACK BELT TIP

When my girls want homemade cinnamon rolls for breakfast and I don't want to wake up with the birds to make them, I make the dough the night before. After the first rise, you can stick the dough in the fridge, and by the next morning, it will be ready to roll out and fill! See Step 6.

BEIGNETS

MAKES 24

1 stick salted butter
1 (8-ounce) block cream cheese
½ cup lukewarm water
½ cup granulated sugar, divided
1 (0.25-ounce) package rapid-rise instant yeast
6 cups all-purpose flour
1 teaspoon salt
1 cup whole milk
2 large eggs
Vegetable oil, for frying
Confectioners' sugar

1. Let the butter and cream cheese sit out for 1 hour.

2. In a small bowl, mix the ½ cup lukewarm water, 1 tablespoon granulated sugar, and yeast. Let stand for about 10 minutes.

3. In the bowl of a stand mixer fitted with the paddle attachment, beat the flour, salt, and remaining granulated sugar at low speed for about 2 minutes.

4. Switch to the dough kneading attachment. Add the yeast mixture, butter, cream cheese, milk, and eggs to the dry ingredients. Beat at low speed for about 3 minutes. Turn the mixer off, and use a flat utensil to scrape the sides and bottom of the bowl. Turn the mixer back on, and let the dough kneader do its thing for another 5 minutes or until you see all ingredients are mixed well and the dough is smooth and not sticking to the sides.

5. Spray a large bowl with cooking spray.

6. Mold the dough into somewhat of a ball, place in the bowl, and cover with a damp towel. Let the dough stand for at least 2 hours on the counter or in the refrigerator overnight to allow the dough to rise.

7. After the dough has risen, in a large skillet, get 2 inches of oil heated to 350° over a medium heat.

8. Dust a flat surface with some flour, and punch down dough on the floured surface, flipping dough so both sides are dusted with flour. Roll the dough to about ¼ inch in thickness. Trim the edges with a pizza cutter if you want to keep all your beignets as squares. Use the same pizza cutter to cut your beignets into 3-inch squares.

9. Before frying, set up a large baking sheet that is layered with paper towels.

10. Drop the beignets in the oil one at a time. You will see them begin to puff up quickly. Once you begin to see some browning forming on the edges, that's when you flip them. Let them fry a little more so each side is golden. Begin removing each beignet, and place on the paper towels. Sift confectioners' sugar over each beignet. Serve and enjoy!

My girls may look sweet here, but they can tear up a plate of beignets!

BANANA BREAD

MAKES 1 (9X5-INCH) LOAF

5   very ripe bananas
1   (14-ounce) can sweetened condensed milk
1½   cups all-purpose flour
½   cup granulated sugar
⅓   cup vegetable oil
¼   cup firmly packed light brown sugar
2   large eggs
1   teaspoon baking soda
1   teaspoon baking powder
1   teaspoon ground cinnamon
1   teaspoon banana extract
½   teaspoon salt

1. Start out by preheating the oven to 350°.

2. In the bowl of a stand mixer fitted with the paddle attachment, mash up the bananas. Add the condensed milk, flour, granulated sugar, oil, brown sugar, eggs, baking soda, baking powder, cinnamon, banana extract, and salt. Beat at medium speed until well combined, about 2 minutes.

3. Grease a 9x5-inch loaf pan. Pour the batter into the pan.

4. Bake for roughly 1 hour and 20 minutes. Let cool for 15 to 20 minutes. Enjoy!

My little sister, Sarah, was the one who encouraged me to come up with a banana bread recipe. You'll be thanking her soon, too!

BLACK BELT TIP

I wait until my bananas are very ripe with a good amount of brown spots before I use them for banana bread. That way, your bread has a strong banana flavor. A little banana extract helps, too. If you want to add nuts, do it! Some walnuts or pecans would be great.

3 | *SNACK ATTACK*
FRIED FAVORITES, BITES, AND BREADS

MINIATURE CRAWFISH PIES

MAKES 34

1 stick salted butter
½ cup all-purpose flour
1 tablespoon olive oil
2 yellow onions, chopped
2 stalks celery, chopped
1 green bell pepper, chopped
1 (10-ounce) can mild diced tomatoes with green chiles, drained
1 tablespoon minced garlic
1 cup chicken broth
½ pint heavy whipping cream
2 pounds crawfish tails
1 tablespoon Pi-YAHHHHH!! Seasoning
1 tablespoon dried parsley
1 teaspoon ground black pepper
1 teaspoon Worcestershire sauce
34 miniature tart piecrusts
Paprika (optional)
Garnish: chopped fresh parsley

1. Start out by heating a large pot and a large pan over a medium-low heat.

2. Preheat your oven to 325°.

3. Melt the butter in the large pot and then add the flour. Stir regularly. You want to get your roux to a peanut butter color. So, if you get there quickly, just turn your heat off until you're ready to add your vegetables.

4. In the large pan, add the oil, and drop in your onion, celery, and bell pepper. Sauté for 20 minutes. You want to be consistent in going back and forth between your roux and vegetables. Add the tomatoes and garlic to your vegetables. Cook for another 5 minutes. Add the chicken broth, and let simmer until you've got your roux to a peanut butter color.

5. Once you've reached the desired color for your roux, slowly add in your vegetable mixture. Mix well. Add the cream. Mix until you see a creamy texture. Add the crawfish, Pi-YAHHHHH!! Seasoning, dried parsley, black pepper, and Worcestershire, and mix well. Turn your heat off, and remove from the heat.

6. Fill each piecrust one spoonful at a time so they get equal amounts. Top them off with a sprinkle of paprika (if using), and place on a baking sheet.

7. Bake for 1 hour or until you see golden edges. Let cool for 10 minutes. Garnish with fresh parsley, if desired, and enjoy!

Leftover crawfish from a crawfish boil make for some of the best next day dishes, like Miniature Crawfish Pies. If anyone sarcastically asks you, "Leftover crawfish? What's that?" you just politely let them know, "If you ain't got leftovers, then you didn't cook enough, and somebody left hungry."

CREAMY CAJUN GUACAMOLE DIP

MAKES 3 CUPS

5   ripe avocados, halved, pitted, and peeled
1   ripe Roma tomato, diced
1   jalapeño, seeded and diced
¼   cup minced red onion (optional)
3   tablespoons chopped fresh cilantro (optional)
½   lime or lemon, juiced
½   tablespoon Pi-YAHHHHH!! Seasoning
1   (8-ounce) package cream cheese, softened
Corn chips, to serve
Garnish: fresh cilantro leaves, minced red onion, diced jalapeño

1. In a large bowl, add the avocados, tomato, jalapeño, red onion (if using), chopped cilantro (if using), lime or lemon juice, and Pi-YAHHHHH!! Seasoning. Blend together. Add the cream cheese, and continue blending. Once all ingredients are mixed well, you're ready to serve with corn chips and enjoy. Garnish with cilantro leaves, red onion, and jalapeño, if desired.

This is Horace Trahan, the famous zydeco and Cajun artist behind the music in most of my videos. He is the front man of the band Horace Trahan and the Ossun Express. Ossun is a small community in Louisiana between Scott and Carencro.

BLACK BELT TIP

This guacamole is all about personal preference. If you like red onion and cilantro, add it. If you don't, skip it. As I always say, you deux you!

CAJUN CAVIAR

MAKES 10 TO 12 SERVINGS

2 (8-ounce) packages cream cheese, softened
1 bunch green onions, finely chopped
1 (8-ounce) block sharp Cheddar cheese, shredded (about 2 cups)
2 cups chopped pecans
1 teaspoon Pi-YAHHHHH!! Seasoning
1 (10-ounce) jar mild jalapeño pepper jelly
Disposable gloves to use for molding
Wheat Thins, to serve

1. In the bowl of a stand mixer fitted with the paddle attachment, beat the cream cheese at low speed. Once you see the cream cheese start to get creamy, add the green onion, cheese, pecans, and Pi-YAHHHHH!! Seasoning. Turn the mixer off, and scrape the sides back toward the center. Turn the mixer back on. You may have to repeat this a couple times until the ingredients are blended evenly.

2. Using disposable gloves, scoop out all the mixture from the mixer bowl, and shape into a ball. Place on the center of a large serving plate, and cover with your desired amount of jalapeño pepper jelly. Surround with Wheat Thins, and enjoy.

Misty and I love Halloween, mostly because it's a reason to have a gathering with friends. We absolutely love having company over. I generally cook up a big ole pot of chili and some hot dogs. Of course, there are often some appetizers along the way. Cajun Caviar has always been one that goes over very well. There's just so much Louisiana flare to it, it's one you have to try.

BLACK BELT TIP

This is one of those snacks that you just can't stop eating. I always serve it with Wheat Thins. You can use the cracker of your choice, but make sure it's sturdy enough!

EGG ROLLS

MAKES ABOUT 40 EGG ROLLS

Peanut oil
1   pound ground beef
1   pound hot blend breakfast sausage
1   yellow onion, chopped
1   bunch green onions, chopped
2   stalks celery, chopped
½   tablespoon Pi-YAHHHHH!! Seasoning
1   teaspoon garlic powder
½   teaspoon salt
½   teaspoon ground black pepper
1   small head cabbage
2   tablespoons garlic-chile sauce
2   tablespoons soy sauce
2   (16-ounce) packages egg roll wraps
Garlic-chile sauce and soy sauce, to serve

1. Start out by adding a small amount of peanut oil to a large pot over a medium-low heat. Let the oil coat across the bottom. Add your beef and sausage to the pot. Cook until there is a mix of brown and pink. Add your yellow onion, green onion, and celery. Add the Pi-YAHHHHH!! Seasoning, garlic powder, salt, and pepper. Cover and cook down, stirring occasionally, for 20 to 30 minutes.

2. Cut your cabbage into quarters, discard the stems, and slice the cabbage into small strips. Place in a bowl on the side for now.

3. Drain meat mixture in a sieve over a plate of paper towels. Add the meat mixture back to the pot, and discard the paper towels.

4. Fold the cabbage into the meat mixture. It will seem like a lot of cabbage, but it will cook down.

5. In a small bowl, mix together your garlic-chile sauce and soy sauce and then pour evenly into the pot. Stir and then cover. Cook over a low heat for roughly 1 hour, checking about every 5 minutes, until the cabbage is completely soft. Turn the heat off, move the mixture to a bowl, and put in the freezer to cool down. If you plan to do the egg rolls the next day, you can move them to the refrigerator. When mixture has cooled (may take an hour), you will begin wrapping.

6. You'll need a bowl of water and a pastry or basting brush. Sometimes it's safe to save one egg roll wrap to test the oil. Brush one corner of a wrap with water and then follow the directions on the egg roll wrap package on how to wrap an egg roll. It's a personal preference on how much stuffing you put per egg roll. I usually do about 2 full tablespoons. About midway through wrapping egg rolls, you want to heat up about ½ inch of peanut oil in a large frying pan to about 350°. (You don't want too much oil, because if the egg rolls are able to float, they will be hard to flip.) Before frying, use the leftover wrap to test your oil to make sure the oil is not too hot.

7. When you are done wrapping, drop the egg rolls, one at a time, into the frying pan. When you start to see a golden color forming on all sides, flip them. Monitor each egg roll from there by flipping. Once they have a nice golden color all around, remove and set in a large dish layered with paper towels. Let cool for a few minutes. Serve with garlic-chile sauce and soy sauce, and enjoy!

TALES FROM THE BAYOU

If you know anything about Jiu-Jitsu, you know that rolling is a big deal. In Brazilian Jiu-Jitsu, "rolling" is a term used for sparring or practicing movements. People who engage in Jiu-Jitsu will even have terms such as "flow rolling" (less intensity) or "hard rolling" (high intensity). If the instructor mentions hard rolls at the beginning of class, be prepared to be sore the next day. Egg Rolls would qualify as a flow roll. LOL. It is a tremendous honor to train with Sensei Scotty Smith and the rest of the team at Next Generation Martial Arts in Thibodaux.

FRIED ONION STRINGS

MAKES 6 SERVINGS

4 medium yellow onions
2 large eggs
1 gallon peanut oil
1 cup all-purpose flour
2 tablespoons Pi-YAHHHHH!! Seasoning,
   plus more to taste
Ketchup, rémoulade sauce, or my Seafood Dip
   (recipe on page 34), to serve

1. Cut off the ends of your onions. Remove the first layer of the onions by cutting a thin line on the outer layer and then peeling it off. Thinly slice the onions. Gently pat the onions dry with some paper towels to remove moisture.

2. In a large bowl, whisk the eggs. Add the onions, mixing well. Let the onions sit.

3. Heat the oil over a medium-low heat in a frying pot that has a basket to easily remove. It's a good idea to have something that can gauge the temperature of the oil so you know how fast the oil is heating.

4. In another large bowl, mix the flour and Pi-YAHHHHH!! Seasoning.

5. When you see that the oil is close to 350°, you can begin battering the onions. You want to be able to drop the onions in the pot right after you batter them up. To batter, remove the onions from the eggs, one at a time, letting the excess drip off, and dredge in the flour mixture, shaking off the excess. Immediately drop into the hot oil.

6. Fry up the onions, in 4 batches, until they start to look golden, 6 to 8 minutes. Remove from the pot, and let drain on some paper towels for a couple minutes. Season with a little more Pi-YAHHHHH!! Seasoning; serve with ketchup, rémoulade, or Seafood Dip, and enjoy!

TALES FROM THE BAYOU

I decided one day to make these when we had too many onions. I didn't feel like spending time making a few different dishes, so I sliced them up, dipped them in egg, and coated them in a homemade batter. My girls tore them up; I could barely eat any myself. These things go great as a side, on top of a burger, or just as a snack by themselves. So, if you've got too many onions, no worries—make some onion strings. These go over very well with my family, and they are so easy to make.

OYSTERS BIENVILLE

MAKES 6 SERVINGS

3   sticks salted butter, divided
1   (8-ounce) package fresh white button mushrooms, chopped
1   pound peeled and deveined fresh Gulf shrimp, chopped
1   yellow onion, minced
1   red bell pepper, minced
1   bunch green onions, minced
1   bunch fresh parsley, minced
1   cup all-purpose flour
2   tablespoons minced garlic
½   pint heavy whipping cream
1   tablespoon Pi-YAHHHHH!! Seasoning
¼   cup dry white wine
24 large oysters on half shell or 48 small oysters on half shell
Plain bread crumbs
Freshly grated Parmesan cheese
French bread, to serve

1. Start out by heating a large sauté pan over a medium to medium-low heat.

2. In your sauté pan, melt 1 stick of butter. Add the mushrooms, and sauté for 5 to 10 minutes.

3. Add the shrimp to your mushrooms. Cook until the shrimp are lightly pink, about 2 minutes. Drain the shrimp and mushroom mixture in a colander over a large bowl. Keep the reserved drippings and the shrimp and mushroom mixture off to the side for now.

4. Wipe down the sauté pan so that no remaining shrimp or mushrooms are left in the pan.

5. In the same pan, melt ½ stick of butter over a low heat. Drop in the yellow onion, bell pepper, green onion, and parsley. Sauté for 25 to 30 minutes.

6. At this time, feel free to preheat your oven to 350°.

7. Add remaining 1½ sticks of butter to the onion mixture. After your butter has fully melted, blend in the flour. Keep blending until you have a blonde roux. Add the garlic, and cook for about 5 minutes. Add the cream. It should be a thick, pasty mixture, so make sure the heat isn't too high. Pour in the liquid from the shrimp and mushroom mixture. Add the Pi-YAHHHHH!! Seasoning. Add the wine, and stir well. Stir in the shrimp and mushrooms. Turn the heat off, set mixture aside, and let cool.

8. Begin laying out fresh oysters on some half shells.

9. Place a spoonful of the vegetable and shrimp mixture on top of each oyster. Stir together bread crumbs and Parmesan, and sprinkle over the top of the vegetable and shrimp mixture.

10. Bake for 20 minutes. Let cool for 5 minutes. Slice you up some French bread, and dive in!

BLACK BELT TIP

If you don't want to use oysters on the half shell, a heatproof oyster pan or baking sheet will work great, too. You can also cook these on the grill, but cook time will vary.

SWEET CAKEY CORNBREAD

MAKES 1 (13X9-INCH) LOAF

12 ounces yellow cake mix (see Black Belt Tip)
1 (12-ounce) package cornbread mix
1 stick salted butter, melted
2 cups whole milk
⅓ cup vegetable oil
3 large eggs
Softened salted butter, to serve

1. Preheat the oven to 350°.

2. Pour the cake mix and cornbread mix into the bowl of stand mixer fitted with the paddle attachment. Turn the mixer on low speed, and make sure the ingredients blend evenly for about 2 minutes. Add the melted butter, milk, oil, and eggs. Mix ingredients for about 5 minutes.

3. Spray the inside of a 13x9-inch baking dish with cooking spray. Pour the batter into the dish.

4. Bake for 30 to 40 minutes or until you see some browning on the edges and a wooden pick comes out clean. Let cool for 5 minutes. Serve with butter, and enjoy.

BLACK BELT TIP

Most boxes of yellow cake mix come in at around 15 ounces, but you'll want to only use 12 ounces of the mix. You can save the remaining mix to make a simple coffee mug cake!

TALES FROM THE BAYOU

When my wife and I were merely boyfriend and girlfriend, we splurged one weekend dining at Emeril Lagasse's restaurant in New Orleans. They served a complementary appetizer of cornbread, and ever since that first bite, I've been chasing the flavor of it. It was sweet and cakey yet still savory and gritty like cornbread. I've never been able to forget it.

One day, I decided to combine a cornbread mix and yellow cake mix with a set amount of ingredients for baking. The result was exactly what I had been searching for—a sweet yet savory, moist cornbread. I know that there are many people who may have a problem with sweet cornbread, but it's not as sweet as you might think. It's just right. All I can say is, give this one a try. You might discover something new about yourself.

Misty and I got married in 2009, and we've been having fun ever since.

JALAPEÑO CRAWFISH CORNBREAD

MAKES 1 (13X9-INCH) LOAF

1½ sticks salted butter, divided
1   yellow onion, chopped
1   green bell pepper, chopped
1   red bell pepper, chopped
1   bunch green onions, chopped
2   jalapeños, halved and seeded, membranes discarded
1   tablespoon minced garlic
1   pound crawfish tails
½   tablespoon Pi-YAHHHHH!! Seasoning
1   (16-ounce) package frozen cream-style corn, thawed
1½ cups yellow cornmeal
½   cup all-purpose flour
1   tablespoon baking powder
½   teaspoon baking soda
3   large eggs
1   pint heavy whipping cream
2   cups shredded sharp Cheddar cheese

1. Start out by heating a large sauté pan on a low heat.

2. Put 1 stick of butter in the freezer.

3. To the sauté pan, add the remaining ½ stick of butter. As the butter begins to melt, raise the heat to a medium heat. Once the butter has melted, add the yellow onion, bell peppers, green onion, and jalapeños, and begin stirring. Sauté the vegetables for roughly 30 minutes.

4. At this point, preheat the oven to 375°.

5. Add the garlic to the vegetable mixture, and sauté for another 5 minutes. Add the crawfish and Pi-YAHHHHH!! Seasoning, and blend evenly. Turn the heat off, mix in the corn, and let sit for now.

6. To the bowl of a stand mixer fitted with the paddle attachment, add the cornmeal, flour, baking powder, and baking soda. Turn the mixer to a low setting, and let mix for about 2 minutes.

7. Meanwhile, take the butter from the freezer, and shred it with a cheese grater. Sprinkle the butter into the mixer. Add the eggs, and let it mix for about 2 minutes.

8. Turn the mixer off. Add the crawfish filling and cream to the bowl. Turn the mixer to a low setting. Sprinkle in the cheese, and mix for about 2 minutes.

9. Spray a 13x9-inch baking dish with cooking spray. Pour in the batter.

10. Bake for 50 minutes or up to 1 hour, depending on your oven calibration, or until it is set. Let cool for 10 minutes. Serve, and enjoy!

FRIED CHICKEN TENDERS

MAKES 6 TO 8 SERVINGS

2 pounds fresh chicken tenderloins
1 cup whole buttermilk
2 tablespoons Pi-YAHHHHH!! Seasoning, divided
1 tablespoon hot sauce
1 gallon peanut oil
2 cups all-purpose flour
Salt and ground black pepper, to taste
French fries, Texas toast, and Seafood Dip (recipe on page 34) or your favorite dipping sauce, to serve

1. The day before, combine the chicken, buttermilk, 1 tablespoon Pi-YAHHHHH!! Seasoning, and hot sauce in a resealable plastic bag. Refrigerate overnight.

2. When ready to fry, pour a few inches' worth of peanut oil into a fry pot. Turn the heat to a medium-high heat. Let the oil gradually get to 375°.

3. In a large bowl or batter box, thoroughly mix the flour and remaining 1 tablespoon Pi-YAHHHHH!! Seasoning.

4. Remove the chicken from the refrigerator, and set aside.

5. When the oil is close to hitting 375°, that is when you want to batter and fry. Batter about 4 pieces of chicken at a time. Remove from the marinade, shaking off excess, and dredge in the flour mixture. Immediately fry as soon as you've battered the chicken.

6. Fry for 6 to 7 minutes or until golden. Make sure you check your temperature so it is not dropping too much. Remove the chicken, and place on a plate layered with paper towels. Season with salt and pepper if you feel necessary. Serve with a side of fries, Texas toast, and Seafood Dip or your favorite dipping sauce. Enjoy!

This was me and my li'l Zoey Jane boarding up for a hurricane. (I know, corny dad rhyme. LOL.) She's been my li'l tagalong since she was a baby. Hurricanes are no fun, but somehow, Louisianans make the best of crummy situations. These fried chicken tenders are a real treat when the power is out and outdoor cooking is all you have.

BOUDIN BALLS

MAKES ABOUT 33

1 (3- to 4-pound) pork shoulder
1 pound pork liver
1½ tablespoons Pi-YAHHHHH!! Seasoning, divided, plus more to season meat
2 tablespoons vegetable oil
2 yellow onions, chopped
2 stalks celery, chopped
1 green bell pepper, chopped
1 bunch green onions, chopped
2 chicken bouillon cubes
2 tablespoons minced garlic
1 (32-ounce) container chicken stock
1 tablespoon dried parsley
1 tablespoon hot sauce
2 cups long-grain white rice
1 cup water
Cayenne pepper (optional)
⅔ gallon cooking oil (preferably peanut)
1 cup all-purpose flour
2 large eggs, lightly beaten, plus more if needed
1 cup panko bread crumbs, plus more if needed
Seafood Dip (recipe on page 34) or ranch dressing, to serve

Food grinder or food grinding attachment for a stand mixer

1. Start out by heating a large pot over a medium heat.

2. Season all sides of the pork and liver with Pi-YAHHHHH!! Seasoning. Set aside for now.

3. In the hot pot, add the vegetable oil. Add the pork shoulder to the pot, and sear for 5 to 6 minutes on each side. Remove the pork, and place in a bowl on the side.

4. Add the liver to the pot, and cook until browned on all sides. (The liver may not have a pleasing smell, but it all comes together in the end). Remove the liver.

5. Add the yellow onion, celery, bell pepper, and green onion to the pot, and sauté for 20 minutes. Add ½ tablespoon Pi-YAHHHHH!! Seasoning and bouillon cubes. Sauté the vegetables for about 20 minutes.

6. Add the minced garlic to the pot, and sauté for another 5 minutes. Pour a small amount of the chicken stock in the pot. Stir around to break up anything stuck to the bottom. Pour in about half of the chicken stock; add the pork shoulder and liver back to the pot. Pour in the remaining chicken stock. Add the parsley and hot sauce. Raise the heat, and bring to a slight boil; cover and lower to a simmer. Cook until tender, about 2 hours.

7. Gently remove the meat from the pot, and place in a bowl on the side. Strain the remaining liquid through a fine-mesh sieve over a bowl to reserve the liquid. Save the vegetables left in the sieve in a bowl to the side for now.

8. In a separate pot, add 3 cups of the reserved liquid, rice, and 1 cup water. Turn the heat on high, and bring to a boil. Once you've reached a boil, cover, lower to a simmer, and cook for 25 minutes. Turn the heat off, and let sit, covered, for another 5 minutes.

9. During this time, hook up the food grinder attachment to your mixer. Turn the mixer on a low setting. Slowly start adding the meat and pushing it down into the food grinder. You may have to cut the meat into smaller pieces for it to fit into your food grinder. Be sure to have a pot or bowl ready to catch everything coming out. Once you've ground up all the meat, add the strained vegetables, and mix well. Let this sit until the rice is done.

10. Once the rice is done, you can then add it to the ground meat mixture. Mix well.

11. Add cayenne (if using) to the remaining reserved liquid. Evenly pour a little of the reserved liquid (about ½ to ⅔ cup) over the meat, gently folding the meat and rice so that the liquid mixes well. The mixture should be sticking together and should be able to be formed into balls. Cover with some foil, and freeze for up to 1 hour.

12. As you're approaching the 1-hour mark, in a 5-quart pot, begin heating up the cooking oil to roughly 350°.

13. Have three bowls set out: one for the flour, one for the eggs, and one for the panko bread crumbs. Add remaining 1 tablespoon Pi-YAHHHHH!! Seasoning to the flour, and mix well.

14. Remove the meat and rice mixture from the freezer. Begin scooping out enough to make balls that are twice the size of a golf ball.

15. Once you have your scoop compressed into a ball, gently roll the ball in the flour and then the egg and then the panko bread crumbs. Set the ball aside, and make 5 more. As you continue on, the egg and panko bowls may need refills, so just be sure to have more on hand.

16. Check the cooking oil to make sure it's around 350°.

17. Gently drop each ball with a pair of tongs into the cooking oil. You will only need to fry for roughly 3 to 5 minutes or until you see the balls are golden in color.

18. After you fry them all up, make sure the last few cool for 5 minutes. Serve with Seafood Dip or ranch dressing, and enjoy!

TALES FROM THE BAYOU

If you're not from Louisiana, you may be wondering what boudin is. Boudin (pronounced "boo-dan") is a sausage made from things like pork, rice, the trinity, and seasonings stuffed into a natural casing, and it's a big deal where I'm from. It's considered a spinoff of French sausages called boudin blanc and boudin noir and dates back a few centuries to when Acadians came to Louisiana from France and Nova Scotia. It's sold everywhere in Louisiana—grocery stores, restaurants, gas stations, you name it—and everyone seems to

have a favorite. There are many that I like, and here in Thibodaux, Big Mike's BBQ makes a great one. If you're not local and can't get boudin in your town, there are a few spots that will ship it to your front door. When it comes to eating boudin, the casing is edible, but when it's steamed or boiled, it gets chewy. So, I like to bite down on a link and pull out the filling with my teeth. My girls love it, too, so much so that I even drop some in with the fixin's in my Crawfish Boil (page 21). These Boudin Balls pack in all of the flavors of traditional boudin into a crispy fried bite!

CRAWFISH BREAD

MAKES 6 TO 8 SERVINGS

2 pounds Louisiana crawfish tails
1 tablespoon Pi-YAHHHHH!! Seasoning
1 teaspoon liquid crab boil
1 stick salted butter
1 yellow onion, chopped
1 green bell pepper, chopped
1 red bell pepper, chopped
1 stalk celery, chopped
1 bunch green onions, chopped
1 tablespoon minced garlic
1 tablespoon dried parsley
8 ounces Velveeta, cubed
1 cup shredded jalapeño Havarti
1½ cups shredded mozzarella
½ cup mayonnaise
1 to 2 large loaves French bread (see Black Belt Tip)

1. Start out by heating a large pot on a low heat.

2. Season the crawfish with the Pi-YAHHHHH!! Seasoning and liquid crab boil. Move to the refrigerator for now.

3. Add the butter to the hot pot. As soon as you see the butter begin to melt, raise the heat to a medium heat. Once the butter has melted, add the yellow onion, bell peppers, celery, and green onion to the pot. Sauté, stirring every so often, for roughly 25 minutes.

4. Add the minced garlic and parsley to the vegetable mixture. Sauté for another 5 minutes.

5. At this time, preheat your oven to 350°.

6. Add the crawfish, Velveeta cubes, jalapeño Havarti, and 1 cup mozzarella to the pot. Slowly stir so that all cheese melts together. Once the cheese has completely melted, mix in the mayonnaise. Blend evenly, and turn the heat off.

7. Cut your French bread in half; slice down the middle of each half. Place the French bread on a large baking sheet. Use 2 baking sheets if you have 2 loaves.

8. Scoop large spoonfuls of the crawfish mixture onto the French bread. Sprinkle the remaining mozzarella cheese over the top.

9. Bake for 10 to 12 minutes. Let cool for 5 minutes. Slice and enjoy!

BLACK BELT TIP

If you spread the crawfish mixture on thick, you'll have enough for 1 loaf, but if you want to make 2 loaves, spread a thinner layer on each. This is a great, filling snack to make for game days!

We Louisianans love our Saints. Football season is the perfect time of year for us to come together and cheer on our favorite team. It doesn't get better than food, friends, and football.

4 | *STIR DA POT*
SOUPS, STEWS, AND GUMBOS

AFTER BOIL SOUP

MAKES ABOUT 13 CUPS

All da fixin's left over from a crawfish boil (sausage, onions, garlic, celery, corn, carrots, mushrooms, potatoes, etc.) (see Black Belt Tip)
1½ sticks salted butter
½ cup all-purpose flour
1 tablespoon vegetable oil
2 (14.5-ounce) cans chicken broth
2 (10.5-ounce) cans cream of mushroom soup
2 quarts half-and-half
1 tablespoon Worcestershire sauce
1 tablespoon hot sauce
1 to 2 pounds crawfish tails left over from a boil
2 cups whole milk
Thick crackers or toasted French bread, to serve

1. Start out by heating a large pot and pan over a low heat.

2. Cut up leftover fixin's according to your desired consistencies. Make sure you at least slice the sausage and chop the onions.

3. In the large pot, add the butter, and increase the heat to a medium-low. Mix in the flour. Stir consistently for roughly 30 minutes

or until you reach a peanut butter color roux. Should you reach the peanut butter color quickly, just turn the heat off.

4. Meanwhile in the large pan, add oil, and drop in the leftover sausage. Sear the sausage until you see it start to brown a little. Move to a bowl, and set aside.

5. Add the leftover onion and celery to the pan. Sauté for a few minutes. (You won't need to sauté for very long; they should already be soft from having been boiled.)

6. Add the first can of broth to the pan. Mash 6 to 7 leftover cloves of garlic, and blend into pan. Add the second can of broth. Add the contents of the pan to the pot with the roux. Blend evenly. Add the sausage, mushrooms, and soup, and stir. Next, add the half-and-half, Worcestershire sauce, and hot sauce, and stir. Raise the heat, and bring to a slight boil. Once you've reached a slight boil, cover, lower to a simmer, and cook for 1 hour.

7. Add the crawfish, milk, potatoes, carrots, corn, or any other soft vegetables you may have had in your boil to the pot. Bring the heat back up to a slight boil; cover, lower to a simmer, and let cook for another 25 to 30 minutes. Serve and enjoy!

BLACK BELT TIP

Don't worry about the amount of fixin's you have or don't have left over from your crawfish boil. Whether you have a little or a lot, this soup will work. Trussme. You can get my Crawfish Boil recipe on page 21.

CHICKEN AND SAUSAGE GUMBO

MAKES 20 CUPS

2   whole rotisserie chickens
3   (32-ounce) containers chicken stock
⅔   cup vegetable oil
1   cup all-purpose flour
1   yellow onion, chopped
1   green bell pepper, chopped
3   stalks celery, chopped
2   tablespoons minced garlic
2   pounds smoked sausage, sliced
2   cups water
1   tablespoon Pi-YAHHHHH!! Seasoning
1   teaspoon salt
1   teaspoon garlic powder
3   dried bay leaves
¼   teaspoon cayenne pepper (optional)
1   (16-ounce) bottle cold water (2 cups)
Hot cooked rice, to serve
Garnish: sliced green onion

1. Pull apart the chicken. Save the remaining skin and bones in a bowl off to the side. Put chicken in the refrigerator.

2. In a pot off to the side, add the chicken stock and the skin and bones from the chicken; cover and heat over a low heat. Just let this simmer until needed.

3. Heat a large pot over a medium heat. Add the oil and then the flour to the hot pot. Begin stirring frequently until you reach a chocolate color. Times will vary on how long it takes to get the roux to a chocolate color, but it usually takes more than 1 hour.

4. When the roux gets to a caramel color, you want to begin draining the stock through a sieve. This way, you can separate all the chicken remains from the stock. Add the stock back to the pot, cover, and let simmer.

5. Once you've reached a good chocolate color, add the yellow onion, bell pepper, celery, and minced garlic to the roux, and cook for another 10 minutes.

6. Meanwhile, heat a large pan over a medium heat. Begin searing your sausage in the pan, just to brown it a little. Once it has browned some, add some of the chicken stock to loosen up any drippings from the sausage. Pour the liquid from the pan through a sieve into the stock.

7. After 10 minutes of cooking the vegetables, ladle in a little bit of the chicken stock, and stir. Repeat until you get a creamy mixture and then add the rest of the stock in. Add the sausage, 2 cups water, Pi-YAHHHHH!! Seasoning, salt, garlic powder, bay leaves, and cayenne (if using). Bring to a boil; cover, lower to a simmer, and cook for 1 hour. You can skim any oil that may have risen to the top, or you can leave it. Add the chicken, and simmer for another 1 hour.

8. At the end, turn the heat off, and add the bottle of cold water. Serve with some rice, and garnish with green onion, if desired!

BLACK BELT TIP

The cold bottle of water will cause a quick drop in temperature, enhancing the flavors in the gumbo. Many Cajuns use a similar technique by adding ice to the end of a crawfish boil.

TALES FROM THE BAYOU

Chicken and Sausage Gumbo was the first recipe I ever filmed and put on social media. At the time, my page only had around 400 followers. I had no idea that this video was going to go viral. Had I known this, I might have put a little more effort into this one. The video is actually 6-second clips that I filmed on Snapchat, and I didn't even show my face in them. To this day, it's my highest-viewed piece of content, yet it is the lowest quality.

The morning after I posted the video, I remember waking up and seeing that it had been shared 11 times. I thought, "Wow! That's a lot of shares!" It's funny to think about this now that the video has been shared more than 500,000 times. Numbers are a tricky thing, though. The comments weren't all positive. Gumbo is a controversial dish, to say the least. The negativity was so overwhelming that I almost deleted the page. Crazy, right? Thankfully, as the days went by, more positivity trickled in, and I decided to keep cooking and sharing what I love. If there's anything that this gumbo taught me, it's that if you don't put yourself out there, the good people will never find you. So, follow your passions, and as always, you deux you!

This is my daughter Isabella's favorite dish I make.

SEAFOOD AND OKRA GUMBO

MAKES 20 CUPS

⅔   cup canola oil, plus more as needed
1   cup all-purpose flour
1   yellow onion, chopped
1   green bell pepper, chopped
2   stalks celery, chopped
2   pounds smoked sausage, sliced
2   tablespoons minced garlic
2   (32-ounce) containers seafood stock
4   cups water
1   tablespoon Pi-YAHHHHH!! Seasoning
1   teaspoon salt
1   teaspoon onion powder
1   teaspoon garlic powder
3   dried bay leaves
2   pounds medium fresh shrimp, peeled and deveined
2   teaspoons liquid crab boil
1   pound fresh okra, chopped
1   pound peeled fresh crab claws
1   (16-ounce) bottle cold water (see Black Belt Tip on page 92)
Hot cooked rice, to serve

1. Start out by heating a large pot over medium-low heat.

2. Now, you want to get started on your roux. Add the oil and then the flour to your pot. Begin stirring at a slow pace, and keep stirring for roughly 1½ hours or until you reach a chocolate color. When you reach about a caramel-looking color, you want to start getting a pan heated on a separate burner.

3. Once your roux reaches a chocolate color, you want to add your onion, bell pepper, and celery. Stir well.

4. Add a small amount of oil to your hot pan on the side; add your sausage to the pan. You want to go back and forth stirring the sausage and the roux with vegetables.

5. After about 5 minutes, add your minced garlic to the roux with vegetables. After another 5 minutes, add one of the containers of seafood stock to the roux. The roux will break up, but that's OK; it will all come together when it simmers.

6. Add a small amount of your other container of seafood stock to your sausage, and mix around to break up the bottom of the pan. Add the rest of the stock to the sausage and then pour the contents of the pan into the gumbo pot. Add the 4 cups water, Pi-YAHHHHH!! Seasoning, salt, onion powder, garlic powder, and bay leaves. Bring to a boil. At this point, if you see some of the oil rise to the top, feel free to scoop that up. Once you've discarded the layer of oil, cover and lower heat to a simmer. Simmer for 2 hours.

7. In a large bowl, add your shrimp and the crab boil; mix well with your hands, and refrigerate.

8. Reheat your large pan, add a small layer of oil; add your okra. Sauté the okra until it starts to brown; add it to the gumbo.

9. Once the 2 hours is up, discard the bay leaves and then add the shrimp and crab claws. Let simmer for another 10 to 15 minutes. Add the cold bottle of water. Serve with rice.

Gumbo is a big deal in the Derouen household. We even named one of our dogs Gumbo. He's the one I'm holding.

CHICKEN NOODLE SOUP

MAKES 14 CUPS

2 pounds boneless chicken breast
1½ tablespoons Pi-YAHHHHH!! Seasoning, divided
1 teaspoon garlic powder
2 (32-ounce) containers chicken stock
2 cups water
3 stalks celery, cut into bite-size pieces
3 carrots, peeled and cut into bite-size pieces
1 bunch green onions, chopped
¼ cup chopped fresh parsley
½ stick salted butter
1 large Vidalia onion, chopped
1 tablespoon minced garlic
1 teaspoon salt
2 dried bay leaves
6 ounces wide noodle pasta

1. Start out by heating a pot over a medium-low heat.

2. Cut the chicken breast into cubes. Season the chicken with 1 tablespoon Pi-YAHHHHH!! Seasoning and garlic powder. Cover and refrigerate.

3. Add the chicken stock and 2 cups water to the pot. Add the celery, carrots, green onion, and parsley. Bring to a boil; once you've reached a boil, cover, lower to a simmer, and cook for 1 hour.

4. Heat a large pan over a medium-low heat. Add the butter. Once the butter has melted, drop in the seasoned chicken. Sear the chicken until you see little to no pink. Once you see that the chicken has a nice sear, remove the chicken from the pan, and place in a bowl off to the side.

5. Add the Vidalia onion to the pan, and sauté for 5 to 10 minutes. Add the minced garlic. When you see that the onions are very soft, add a small amount of water to the pan to break up any remnants from the bottom. Pour contents of pan into the pot with all the stock and vegetables. Continue to cook until you reach the 1-hour mark.

6. Once you reach the 1-hour mark, add the chicken, salt, bay leaves, and remaining ½ tablespoon Pi-YAHHHHH!! Seasoning. Bring back up to a boil; cover, lower to a simmer, and let cook for 50 minutes.

7. Add the pasta to the pot, cover, and cook for another 10 minutes.

8. After the last 10 minutes of cooking, taste the pasta to see that the texture is to your liking. If it's still a little hard, just continue to let simmer until it reaches your desired consistency. Once the pasta is fully cooked, shut the heat off and serve. Enjoy!

BLACK BELT TIP

You can use store-bought chicken stock if you want, but my homemade stock on page 37 gives this good-for-you soup even more flavor.

BEEF AND VEGETABLE SOUP

MAKES 24 CUPS

2 to 3 pounds beef stew meat
Kosher salt and ground black pepper, to taste
3 tablespoons vegetable oil
1 yellow onion, chopped
1 green bell pepper, chopped
2 tablespoons minced garlic
1 (32-ounce) container beef broth
2 (46-ounce) bottles tomato or vegetable juice
2 to 3 baking potatoes, cut into large pieces
3 stalks celery, cut into large pieces
3 carrots, peeled and cut into large pieces
1 pound green beans, trimmed
1 head cabbage, white center removed, chopped into large pieces
1 (8-ounce) package sliced fresh mushrooms
1 handful fresh parsley, finely chopped
1 tablespoon Pi-YAHHHHH!! Seasoning
2 dried bay leaves
1 (12-ounce) bag frozen corn
Small shell pasta (optional), cooked according to package directions
Garnish: chopped fresh parsley

1. Start out by heating a large pot over a medium heat.

2. Season the beef stew meat generously with the salt and black pepper.

3. Add the vegetable oil to the large pot, and let coat evenly. Drop the beef in. Cook the beef until you see hardly any pink left. Remove the beef, and place it in a large bowl off to the side.

4. Drop the onion, bell pepper, and garlic into the pot. Sauté the vegetables for 25 minutes, stirring occasionally.

5. Once the sautéed vegetables are soft, add in the beef broth. Next, add the tomato or vegetable juice. Add the cooked beef back in. Add in the potatoes, celery, carrots, green beans, cabbage, mushrooms, and parsley. Add Pi-YAHHHHH!! Seasoning and bay leaves. Bring to a boil; cover, lower to a simmer, and cook for 1 hour.

6. Pour the frozen corn into the pot. Bring back to a boil; cover, lower to a simmer, and cook for another 1 hour. Add your desired amount of pasta (if using) to your bowl, garnish with parsley, if desired, and enjoy.

TALES FROM THE BAYOU

When the weather gets cold, I always like to make this soup. It's meaty and filled with vegetables and seems to warm you up from the inside out. When this photo was taken, Misty and I were in Dallas, Texas. While we were there, there was a huge winter snow—a once-in-1,000-years kind of freeze. We were stuck at our hotel all week, but Misty and I always seem to make the most of any circumstance, and to be honest, I think the angels were looking after us. It was a tough time for most people in the surrounding areas (Southerners don't handle this kind of weather well), but we were lucky enough to have everything we needed at the hotel. But after checking out the snow, we sure could've used a big bowl of this soup.

CORN SOUP

MAKES 24 CUPS

1 pound pork stew meat, cut into large chunks
Kosher salt and ground black pepper, to taste
1 tablespoon vegetable oil
1 pound smoked tasso, cut into large chunks
1 yellow onion, chopped
1 green bell pepper, chopped
2 stalks celery, chopped
1 bunch green onions, chopped
2 tablespoons minced garlic
1 stick salted butter
½ cup all-purpose flour
2 (32-ounce) containers chicken stock, divided
1 (6-ounce) can tomato paste
2 (14.5-ounce) cans stewed tomatoes
1 (28-ounce) can crushed tomatoes
1 (10-ounce) can diced tomatoes with green chiles
1 tablespoon granulated sugar
1 tablespoon Pi-YAHHHHH!! Seasoning
½ tablespoon garlic powder
1 teaspoon salt
3 dried bay leaves
2 cups water
2 (16-ounce) packages frozen sweet creamed corn, thawed
1 (24-ounce) bag frozen corn kernels

1. Start out by heating a large pan over a medium heat.

2. Season the pork generously with kosher salt and black pepper.

3. Add the oil to the hot pan. Drop the pork into the pan. Make sure none of the pieces are on top of each other. Let the pork brown for roughly 15 minutes, stirring occasionally.

4. After 15 minutes of sautéing the pork, add the tasso to the pan, and sear for another 5 minutes. After 5 minutes is up, remove all the meat from the pan, and place in a bowl off to the side.

5. Add the yellow onion, bell pepper, celery, green onion, and minced garlic to the pan, and begin stirring the vegetables around so you bring up any of the drippings from the meat. Continue sautéing for 20 minutes.

6. Meanwhile, get started making a roux. Heat a large pot over a low heat. Add the butter, and let it melt. Increase the heat to a medium-low, and add the flour. Begin stirring immediately. Go back and forth between the roux and the vegetables, stirring frequently.

7. After the vegetables have been sautéing for 20 minutes, add a small amount of chicken stock to the pan. Break up any remaining remnants from the bottom of the pan. Add the rest of that container of chicken stock. Add the pork and tasso. Cover and let simmer until the roux reaches a peanut butter color.

8. Once the roux reaches a peanut butter color, add the tomato paste. Blend into the roux until you get a paste-like mixture.

9. Add the contents of the hot pan to the hot pot, and stir. Next, add in stewed tomatoes, crushed tomatoes, and diced tomatoes with green chiles, and stir. Add the sugar, Pi-YAHHHHH!! Seasoning, garlic powder, salt, and bay leaves, and blend together. Add the 2 cups water and the remaining container of chicken stock. Blend together. Raise the heat so you can bring the soup to a boil. Once you've reached a slight boil, cover, lower to a simmer, and let cook for 1 hour.

10. Add the thawed creamed corn and frozen corn to the pot. Blend together. If you see any bay leaves at this point, feel free to discard them. Raise the heat back up to bring to a slight boil. Once you've reached a slight boil, cover, lower to simmer, and let cook for another 1 hour. After the hour is up, you're ready to serve. Enjoy!

BLACK BELT TIP

Tasso is a smoked pork product that goes into a lot of Cajun cooking. If you can't find it in your own grocery store, search online. There are several spots that will ship it to you.

CORN & CRAWFISH BISQUE

MAKES 16 CUPS

2 sticks salted butter, divided
2 yellow onions, chopped
1 green bell pepper, chopped
2 stalks celery, chopped
1 bunch green onions, chopped
1 tablespoon minced garlic
½ cup all-purpose flour
2 (10-ounce) cans chicken broth
2 quarts half-and-half
2 (14.75-ounce) cans cream-style corn
2 (10.5-ounce) cans cream of mushroom soup
2 (10-ounce) bags frozen corn kernels
1 tablespoon Pi-YAHHHHH!! Seasoning
1 tablespoon Worcestershire sauce
1 tablespoon hot sauce
1 teaspoon ground black pepper
2 pounds fresh local crawfish tails
Thick crackers or French bread, to serve

1. Start out by heating a large pot and a sauté pan over a low heat.

2. Melt ½ stick of butter in the sauté pan. Increase the heat to a medium-low, and drop your yellow onion, bell pepper, celery, green onion, and garlic in.

3. In your large pot, melt remaining 1½ sticks of butter; increase the heat, and blend in the flour, stirring frequently. You're going to want to go back and forth between your pot and pan consistently stirring for about 30 minutes. The idea is to get very soft vegetables and a peanut butter color roux. If one happens to come along faster than the other, turn the heat off to that one burner, and continue to work on the other one.

4. Once you have both a peanut butter color roux and very tender vegetables, stir the chicken broth into the vegetables and then pour the mixture into the pot with the roux. Mix well. Add the half-and-half, and raise your heat to a medium-high. Add the cream-style corn, soup, frozen corn, Pi-YAHHHHH!! Seasoning, Worcestershire, hot sauce, and black pepper. Mix well. Let the heat rise until you see some slight bubbling; lower heat, cover, and let simmer for 30 minutes to 1 hour.

5. Once that time has passed, add your crawfish, and let simmer for another 20 to 30 minutes. Serve with some thick crackers or French bread, and enjoy!

We all love crawfish in this house, including my oldest daughter, Isabella. We call her "Bella" for short.

CHILI WITH BEANS

MAKES 18 CUPS

2   **jalapeños, divided**
1   **tablespoon olive oil, divided**
2   **yellow onions, chopped**
1   **green bell pepper, chopped and seeded**
1   **poblano pepper, chopped and seeded**
1   **(6-ounce) can tomato paste**
1   **tablespoon minced garlic**
2   **pounds ground beef**
1   **cup water**
2   **(15-ounce) cans tomato sauce**
2   **(15-ounce) cans Ranch Style Beans**
2   **(14.5-ounce) can diced tomatoes**
2   **tablespoons cumin**
2   **tablespoons chili powder**
½   **tablespoon garlic salt**
½   **tablespoon smoked paprika**
½   **tablespoon Pi-YAHHHHH!! Seasoning**
2   **dried bay leaves**
Cayenne pepper (optional)
Optional fixin's: hot dogs, corn chips, sour cream, shredded cheese

1. Heat up a large pot and a large pan over a medium heat.

2. Mince 1 jalapeño. Make sure you remove all seeds.

3. Add ½ tablespoon oil to the large pan. Add the minced jalapeño, onion, bell pepper, and poblano pepper. Sauté for 15 to 20 minutes. Add the tomato paste and minced garlic. Sauté for another 10 minutes.

4. Meanwhile, add the remaining ½ tablespoon oil to the large pot, and drop in the ground beef.

5. After 10 minutes of sautéing the vegetables with the paste, add the 1 cup water to the pan, and break up anything stuck to the bottom. Pour the vegetable mixture into the pot with the ground beef. Add the tomato sauce, Ranch Style Beans, and diced tomatoes. Add the cumin, chili powder, garlic salt, smoked paprika, Pi-YAHHHHH!! Seasoning, bay leaves, and cayenne (if using). Mince the remaining jalapeño with the seeds, and add to the pot.

6. Turn the heat up to bring the chili to a slight boil. Once boil is achieved, cover and lower the heat to a simmer. Let simmer for 2 to 3 hours, stirring every 15 minutes. Break out the fixin's, and enjoy!

BLACK BELT TIPS

You may want to use a glove when chopping the jalapeño. The residue from the pepper can wreak havoc on your skin.

There's not much better than a good chili dog, and this chili is great for that. But my family has also been known to serve it over corn chips with plenty of shredded cheese or just ladle it into bowls and top with everyone's favorite fixin's.

CHICKEN FRICASSEE

MAKES 12 CUPS

⅔ cup plus ¼ cup vegetable oil, divided
1 cup all-purpose flour, plus more for coating
4 to 5 pounds chicken legs and thighs
Pi-YAHHHHH!! Seasoning and garlic powder, to taste
1 yellow onion, chopped
1 green bell pepper, chopped
1 bunch green onions, chopped
2 stalks celery, chopped
1 tablespoon minced garlic
1 (32-ounce) container chicken stock
2 cups water
1 tablespoon dried parsley
½ tablespoon salt
1 teaspoon ground black pepper
1 dried bay leaf
Hot cooked rice, to serve
Garnish: chopped fresh parsley

1. Start out by heating a large pot and a large pan over a medium-low heat.

2. Get started on a roux by adding ⅔ cup oil and then flour to the large pot. Begin stirring immediately. You are aiming for a chocolate color roux. This could take more than 1 hour. Once the roux starts to get to a tan, creamy consistency, it's OK to let it sit for a few moments at a time while prepping the chicken (as long as your heat isn't too high).

3. Season both sides of the chicken with generous portions of Pi-YAHHHHH!! Seasoning and garlic powder. Coat both sides of the chicken with flour. Remember to stir the roux in between.

4. In the large pan, add the remaining ¼ cup oil. Add the chicken, skin side down. Brown the chicken for 5 to 8 minutes on each side. (Time depends on how hot your pan is.) Once you've browned both sides of all the chicken, place in a bowl off to the side.

5. Add the yellow onion, bell pepper, green onion, celery, and minced garlic to the pan. Sauté for roughly 30 minutes. If the roux gets to a chocolate color before the vegetables are done, just turn the heat off on the roux. After 30 minutes of sautéing the vegetables, add the chicken stock. Stir the bottom of the pan so you can break up any remaining drippings. Cover and let cook on a simmering heat.

6. Once the roux has reached a chocolate color, turn the heat to a low simmer, and add half of the vegetable mixture to the roux. Begin stirring until you reach a creamy consistency. Add the rest of the vegetable mixture to the pan, and stir. Add the 2 cups water, dried parsley, salt, black pepper, and bay leaf. Blend evenly. Add the chicken to the pot. Be sure to add any remaining liquid left from the bowl of chicken. Raise the heat to high so the pot comes to a slight boil. Once you've reached a slight boil, cover, lower to a simmer, and let cook for 2 hours. Serve with some rice, garnish with fresh parsley, if desired, and enjoy!

TALES FROM THE BAYOU

Chicken Fricassee is pure Cajun comfort food. If you're not familiar with the name, this dish is at its base chicken and gravy. A lot of people call it chicken stew, and some even call it smothered chicken. "Fricassee" is a word with French origin that describes meat that has been slowly stewed in a sauce. Down in these parts, you'll find lots of dishes with French origin, and this just so happens to be one of my favorites and my followers', too. The chicken thighs and legs are tender and juicy, and the rice soaks up every last bit of the brown gravy. No matter what you call it, it hits the spot every time!

BEEF STEW

MAKES 20 CUPS

2 pounds beef stew meat
Salt and ground black pepper, to taste
1 cup plus 1 tablespoon all-purpose flour, divided
2 sticks salted butter
2 tablespoons vegetable oil
1 yellow onion, chopped
2 tablespoons minced garlic
1 bunch celery, chopped
1 bunch carrots, peeled and chopped
1 (32-ounce) container beef stock
2 tablespoons Worcestershire sauce
1 tablespoon dried parsley
½ tablespoon garlic powder
½ tablespoon Pi-YAHHHHH!! Seasoning
2 pounds small red potatoes, quartered
1 cup water
Hot cooked rice or mashed potatoes, to serve
Garnish: chopped fresh parsley

1. Start out by heating a large pot over a low heat and a large pan over a medium heat.

2. Season the beef with generous portions of salt and pepper; dust with 1 tablespoon flour.

3. Start making a roux in the large pot by first melting the butter; raise the heat to a medium-low, and add the remaining 1 cup flour. Continue to stir the roux frequently until you get a chocolate color. This may take up to 1 hour or more.

4. In the meantime, get started searing the beef by adding oil to your large pan and then dropping the beef in. Just remember to always go back and stir the roux. Once the beef has browned up nicely, remove it with a slotted spatula, and place it in a bowl. Add your onion to the drippings. Sauté them for about 25 minutes; halfway through, add the minced garlic.

5. At this point, you can raise the heat to medium on your roux to help speed the process.

6. Once the onions have sautéed down, you can add your celery and carrots. Just let them cook for about another 5 minutes. Add the beef stock. Add the Worcestershire, dried parsley, garlic powder, and Pi-YAHHHHH!! Seasoning. Let simmer until ready to add to the roux.

7. Once your roux has reached a chocolate color, turn the heat off, and let cool for about 5 minutes. Pour your beef stock mixture into the pot with the roux. Turn your heat back up to high.

8. Drop in your beef, potatoes, and 1 cup water. Stir, and bring to a slight boil. Once you have reached the slight boil, cover and let simmer for 2 hours. Serve with some rice or mashed potatoes, garnish with fresh parsley, if desired, and enjoy!

This is my nephew, Elijah. We start 'em early on the Pi-YAHHHHHH!!

TACO SOUP

MAKES 12 CUPS

1   tablespoon vegetable oil
2   pounds ground beef
1   tablespoon Pi-YAHHHHH!! Seasoning
2   yellow onions, chopped
1   green bell pepper, chopped
1   bunch green onions, chopped
1   (10-ounce) can diced tomatoes with green chiles
1   tablespoon minced garlic
1   tablespoon chili powder
1   (1-ounce) package taco seasoning mix
1   (1-ounce) package ranch seasoning mix
2   cups chicken stock
1   (15-ounce) can Ranch Style Beans
1   (12-ounce) bag frozen corn kernels

Optional fixin's: shredded cheese, sliced jalapeños, sliced avocado, sour cream, corn chips

1. Heat a large pot over a medium heat.

2. To the large pot, add the oil. Make sure it coats the bottoms evenly. Drop in the ground beef. Season the beef with the Pi-YAHHHHH!! Seasoning. Cook the beef evenly until it's browned and crumbly. Drain the beef through a sieve sitting on top of a bowl.

3. Take the drippings from the beef, and add them back to the pot. Add the yellow onion, bell pepper, and green onion to the pot. Sauté the vegetables for about 20 minutes. Add the tomatoes and garlic, and sauté for about 10 minutes. Add the chili powder, taco seasoning, and ranch seasoning, and mix well. Add a small amount of the chicken stock to help break up anything stuck to the bottom of the pot. Once broken up, add the ground beef, Ranch Style Beans, and remaining chicken stock. Raise the heat to bring to a slight boil. Once you reach a slight boil, cover the pot, lower to a simmer, and let cook for 1 hour, stirring the bottom every 10 minutes.

4. After the 1-hour mark, add the corn to the pot. Raise the heat to bring to a slight boil. Once a slight boil is reached, cover, lower to a simmer, and let cook for 20 minutes, stirring every 10 minutes. Uncover and cook for another 10 minutes. Serve with any of your favorite fixin's. Enjoy!

BLACK BELT TIP

This soup isn't too spicy, but if you want to heat it up, top with some sliced jalapeños for that extra kick. Mrs. Cajun Ninja and I enjoy a good margarita alongside our Taco Soup.

MEATBALL STEW

MAKES 12 CUPS

Stew:
⅔ cup vegetable oil
1 cup all-purpose flour
2 yellow onions, chopped
1 green bell pepper, chopped
2 stalks celery, chopped
1 bunch green onions, chopped
1 tablespoon minced garlic
1 (32-ounce) container chicken stock (beef broth or stock also works)
4 cups hot water
1 tablespoon Pi-YAHHHHH!! Seasoning
1 tablespoon dried parsley
1 tablespoon Worcestershire sauce
1 teaspoon ground black pepper
2 dried bay leaves

Meatballs:
2 pounds ground beef
1 tablespoon Worcestershire sauce
½ tablespoon Pi-YAHHHHH!! Seasoning
1 teaspoon salt
1 teaspoon garlic powder
1 teaspoon onion powder
Water, as needed
2 slices white bread
1 cup plain bread crumbs
2 large eggs

Hot cooked rice, to serve
Garnish: chopped fresh parsley

1. Start out by heating a large pot over a low heat.

2. For the stew: Add the oil and then the flour to the pot. Begin making the roux by slowly stirring the flour and oil. This is a time-consuming process. You're going to want to stir for up to 1 hour or until you reach a chocolate color. Upon reaching a chocolate color, drop in the yellow onion, bell pepper, celery, and green onion, and sauté for 15 minutes. Add the minced garlic, and sauté for about another 5 minutes.

3. Add the chicken stock to the pot a little at a time. Blend evenly. Add 4 cups hot water. Add the Pi-YAHHHHH!! Seasoning, parsley, Worcestershire sauce, black pepper, and bay leaves, and stir. Bring to a boil; cover, lower to a simmer, and let cook for 1 hour.

4. Preheat your oven to 375°.

5. Meanwhile, for the meatballs: In a large bowl, add the ground beef, Worcestershire, Pi-YAHHHHH!! Seasoning, salt, garlic powder, and onion powder.

6. In a plate off to the side, add a small amount of water. Dampen the bread in the plate, tear the bread into small pieces, and add to the bowl. Add the bread crumbs and eggs. Mix well with your hands. Roll the mixture into meatballs a little larger than the size of a golf ball, and place them on a greased pan.

7. Bake for 25 to 30 minutes. Once the meatballs are done, set aside in a strainer over a plate until the 1-hour mark is up on your stew.

8. Gently add the meatballs, one at a time, to the stew. You can also discard the bay leaves at this point. Bring the stew back to a slight boil; lower heat to a medium-low. Let the stew cook, uncovered, for another 1 hour or until the gravy reaches your desired consistency. Serve with rice, garnish with fresh parsley, if desired, and enjoy!

BLACK BELT TIP
This is a classic dish in the Acadian region of Louisiana. It's a different take on rice and gravy that will blow you away.

CRAWFISH STEW

MAKES 10 CUPS

⅔ cup vegetable oil
1 cup all-purpose flour
2 yellow onions, chopped
1 green bell pepper, chopped
2 stalks celery, chopped
1 bunch green onions, chopped
1 tablespoon minced garlic
5 cups hot water, divided
1 tablespoon Pi-YAHHHHH!! Seasoning (see Black Belt Tips)
1 tablespoon dried parsley
1 teaspoon garlic powder
1 teaspoon ground black pepper
Boiled eggs (optional)
2 pounds crawfish tails
Hot cooked rice and Potato Salad (recipe on page 232), to serve
Garnish: chopped fresh parsley

1. Start out by heating a large pot over a medium-low heat.

2. Add the oil and then the flour to your heated pot. Make a chocolate color roux by stirring constantly with a wooden spoon. This process can take 1 hour or more, so be patient. Once your roux has reached a chocolate color, drop in the yellow onion, bell pepper, celery, and green onion, and stir for another 5 minutes. Add the minced garlic, stir for another about 5 minutes.

3. Add 4 cups hot water to pot. Blend evenly. Add the Pi-YAHHHHH!! Seasoning, parsley, garlic powder, and black pepper. Mix well. Raise the heat to a boil; cover, lower to a simmer, and let cook for 1 hour, stirring every 15 minutes. (Or 1½ hours if you aren't adding eggs.)

4. After the 1-hour mark, add the boiled eggs (if using) to the pot. Let simmer for 30 minutes.

5. Add the crawfish to the pot. Pour remaining 1 cup hot water over the crawfish, and stir. Bring to a slight boil; cover, lower to a simmer, and let cook for another 30 minutes. Serve with rice and Potato Salad, garnish with fresh parsley, if desired, and enjoy!

BLACK BELT TIPS

Down in these parts, it's customary to serve potato salad with crawfish and shrimp stews.

If you're using boiled crawfish, use less seasoning in the stew. If you boiled it right, your crawfish should already have a kick!

SHRIMP AND CRABMEAT STEW

MAKES 14 CUPS

2/3 cup vegetable oil
1 cup all-purpose flour
2 yellow onions, chopped
1 green bell pepper, chopped
2 stalks celery, chopped
1 tablespoon minced garlic
5 cups hot water, plus more if needed
1 tablespoon Pi-YAHHHHH!! Seasoning
1 teaspoon garlic powder
1 teaspoon ground black pepper
2 dried bay leaves
1 bunch green onions, chopped
¼ cup chopped fresh parsley
1 cup lump crabmeat, picked free of shell
2 pounds peeled and deveined medium fresh shrimp
Boiled eggs (optional)
Garnish: sliced green onion

1. Start out by heating a pot over a medium to medium-low heat.

2. Add the oil and then the flour to your pot, and stir immediately. Maintain a slow stir for 1 hour or more until you reach a chocolate color roux. Add your yellow onion, bell pepper, and celery to the roux, and sauté for roughly 5 minutes. Add the minced garlic, and sauté for about another 5 minutes. Be cautious of heat. Lower if necessary.

3. Add the 5 cups hot water to the pot. Stir until blended well. Add the Pi-YAHHHHH!! Seasoning, garlic powder, black pepper, and bay leaves. Blend evenly. Set the pot to a low heat. Add chopped green onion and parsley. Bring to a slight boil; cover, and let cook for 2 hours, stirring every 20 minutes.

4. After the 2-hour mark, if you find it's too thick, you may want to add another 1 cup hot water. Add the crabmeat. Add shrimp and eggs (if using). Raise the heat to a slight boil; cover and lower to a simmer. Cook for 15 minutes. Garnish with sliced green onion, if desired. Serve, and enjoy.

BLACK BELT TIP

Throughout the process, you can add water to maintain your preferred consistency and salt to maintain flavor.

TALES FROM THE BAYOU

This is Kenny Naquin, an old friend of mine from the days when I used to wait tables. He was always there for me any time I needed him. He even lent me money so that I could buy the engagement ring I wanted to get Misty. In late 2018, he was diagnosed with stomach cancer. Misty and I helped throw a benefit for him and got as many people as possible to come out and support Kenny. Today, our prayers have been answered and he is in remission. One of Kenny's favorite dishes that I make is shrimp stew (without the eggs), so I had to dedicate this one to him.

Any chance I get, I love to kayak
and fish on Bayou Lafourche,
a 106-mile-long bayou that runs
through southeast Louisiana.

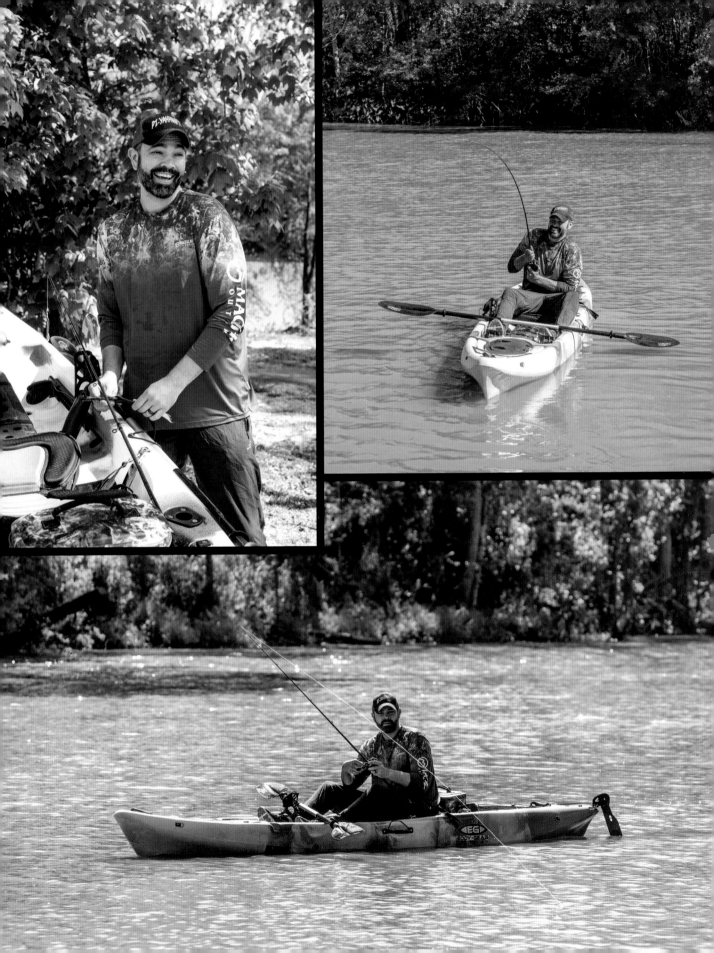

5 | PASTA SUPPERS
REAL GOOD, FEEL-GOOD MEALS

CREAMY CRAWFISH ROTINI

MAKES 6 SERVINGS

1   **stick salted butter**
1   **yellow onion, chopped**
1   **yellow bell pepper, chopped**
1   **bunch green onions, chopped**
1   **pound crawfish tails**
1   **tablespoon minced garlic**
1½ **teaspoons salt, divided**
1   **(16-ounce) package rotini pasta**
1   **pint heavy whipping cream**
½   **tablespoon Pi-YAHHHHH!! Seasoning**
¼   **teaspoon cayenne pepper**

1. Start out by heating a large pan over a low heat. Also, heat up a pot of water over a high heat.

2. Add the butter to the pan. Once the butter has melted, raise the heat to medium-low, and add the yellow onion, bell pepper, and green onion to the pan. Sauté the vegetables for 25 minutes. Add the crawfish and garlic, and continue to sauté for another 5 minutes or until the vegetables are very soft.

3. At this time, your pot of water should be boiling. Add 1 teaspoon salt to the pot of water and then add in the rotini pasta. Boil the pasta for 8 to 9 minutes and then drain.

4. After the crawfish and vegetables have been sautéing for the allotted time, lower the heat to a simmer, and add in heavy cream. Add the Pi-YAHHHHH!! Seasoning, cayenne, and remaining ½ teaspoon salt. Next, add the pasta, and stir well. Cover and continue to simmer for another 15 to 20 minutes. Turn the heat off, and serve. Enjoy!

TALES FROM THE BAYOU

This is my spin on a Bayou State classic—Crawfish Monica. The original Crawfish Monica was created by Chef Pierre Hilzim of Kajun Kettle Foods, who named the dish after his wife, Monica. Now, it's tradition here in south Louisiana. If you've ever been to New Orleans Jazz & Heritage Festival that takes place each spring, you know that Kajun Kettle Foods' Crawfish Monica draws a crowd every year. My homemade version is quick and easy to make. It's creamy and just a tad spicy, and it can be made even on busy weeknights when you're in a rush to get dinner on the table.

SHRIMP FETTUCINE

MAKES 10 SERVINGS

2 pounds peeled and deveined medium fresh shrimp
2 teaspoons liquid shrimp & crab boil
1 tablespoon Pi-YAHHHHH!! Seasoning
1 teaspoon garlic salt
2 sticks salted butter, divided
1 yellow onion, chopped
3 stalks celery, chopped
1 green bell pepper, chopped
1 tablespoon minced garlic
2 (12-ounce) packages fettuccine
1 teaspoon salt
1 (10-ounce) can diced tomatoes with green chiles
1 (10.5-ounce) can cream of chicken soup
1 (14.5-ounce) can chicken broth
1 quart half-and-half
1 (16-ounce) block Velveeta Jalapeño or Velveeta Queso Blanco
Garlic breadsticks, to serve
Garnish: chopped fresh parsley

1. Start out by heating a large pot over a low heat.

2. Season the shrimp with the crab boil, Pi-YAHHHHH!! Seasoning, and garlic salt, and refrigerate until ready to use.

3. Melt 1½ sticks of butter in the pot. When the butter has melted, add the onion, celery, and bell pepper. Raise the heat to medium, and sauté for 20 minutes.

4. Bring a large pot filled more than halfway full of water to a boil.

5. Add the minced garlic to the vegetable mixture, and continue sautéing for another 5 minutes.

6. When the water begins to boil, add the pasta and salt to the water. Boil for 1 minute less than the package directions, drain, and set aside.

7. After the vegetables have cooked for 25 minutes, add the tomatoes. Let cook for another 5 minutes. Add the soup, broth, and half-and-half.

8. Meanwhile, begin heating a sauté pan over a low heat. At this time, preheat the oven to 350°.

9. Cut block of Velveeta into cubes, and add to the sauce mixture, stirring frequently.

10. Add the remaining ½ stick of butter to the sauté pan. When the butter has halfway melted, raise the heat to medium. When the butter has completely melted, add the shrimp to the pan. Sauté for 3 to 4 minutes.

11. While the shrimp are sautéing, add the pasta to the sauce, and stir well. The pasta may be stuck together, but slowly stirring will break it up.

12. After the shrimp are done sautéing, add the shrimp to the sauce, and stir to combine.

13. Divide the mixture into 2 (13x9-inch) baking dishes. Cover with foil.

14. Bake for 15 to 20 minutes. Gently remove the foil. Let cool for 5 minutes. Serve with garlic breadsticks, and garnish with parsley, if desired.

Tim Credeur is a former professional mixed martial artist and current coach from Breaux Bridge, Louisiana. When I first started popping off on social media, he made my shrimp fettucine and tagged me. I hope you like it as much as he did.

BLACK BELT TIP

You can easily freeze one of the pans for later if you want. After you divide the mixture into separate pans, making sure the one you're saving is in a freezer-safe dish, let the mixture cool completely. Next, wrap the casserole tightly in several layers of foil, label it, and pop it into your freezer. When you want to reheat it, pull it out of the freezer and let it thaw in your refrigerator for about a day. Let it stand at room temperature for 30 minutes and then bake, covered, at 350° until it is heated through. You can also swap out the shrimp for crawfish tails to make a crawfish fettucine.

SHRIMP & TASSO PASTA

MAKES 7 SERVINGS

1   **(16-ounce) package bow tie pasta**
1   **stick salted butter**
1   **pound tasso, chopped**
1   **yellow onion, chopped**
1   **red bell pepper, chopped**
1   **stalk celery, chopped**
1   **tablespoon minced garlic**
1   **quart heavy whipping cream**
½   **cup shredded Parmesan cheese, plus more for sprinkling**
½   **tablespoon Pi-YAHHHHH!! Seasoning**
½   **teaspoon salt**
¼   **teaspoon cayenne pepper**
1   **pound peeled and deveined medium fresh shrimp**

1. Start out by cooking your pasta according to the directions; drain, and set aside.

2. While pasta is cooking, heat a large pot over a medium heat.

3. Add the butter to the pot, and let melt. Add tasso, and cook until it gets somewhat of a sear. Remove tasso, and set aside in a bowl. Add the onion, bell pepper, and celery. Let cook for 20 minutes, stirring occasionally.

4. Add the garlic to the vegetable mixture, and cook for another 5 minutes. Add heavy cream, Parmesan, Pi-YAHHHHH!! Seasoning, salt, and cayenne. Mix until cheese has melted. Add the shrimp, and let cook until you start to see them turn pink. Add the tasso back in, and let cook for 5 minutes. Add your pasta. (Pasta may be stuck together, but gradually scooping sauce over pasta will break it up.) Once dish has mixed well, sprinkle with additional Parmesan, and taste to see if you need to add anything. If not, then serve and enjoy.

TALES FROM THE BAYOU

Master Sergeant Ryan Leonard is a United States Marine and one of my closest friends from high school. I was actually there to see him earn the rank of Master Sergeant. This same year, I also earned the rank of Master in Taekwondo. I thought this was really cool because it both took us 20 plus years to achieve.

For a little guy, he sure can eat. I'll never forget when he returned home from boot camp. My mom cooked up a shrimp and bow tie pasta dish. He must have had four plates. Can't blame him, though; he burned an awful lot of calories in boot camp.

PASTALAYA WITH CHICKEN & PORK

MAKES 8 SERVINGS

1 pound pork roast, cut into cubes
Salt and ground black pepper, to taste
¼ cup vegetable oil
1 pound boneless chicken thighs, cut into cubes
1 pound smoked sausage, sliced crosswise
1 yellow onion, chopped
1 green bell pepper, chopped
1 bunch green onions, chopped
2 stalks celery, chopped
3 beef bouillon cubes
½ tablespoon Pi-YAHHHHH!! Seasoning
1 tablespoon minced garlic
3½ cups water
1 (10.5-ounce) can cream of chicken soup
1 tablespoon hot sauce
2 tablespoons browning and seasoning sauce
1 (16-ounce) package bow tie pasta (or favorite pasta)
Garnish: chopped fresh parsley

1. First, start out by heating an oven-safe pot over a medium heat.

2. Season the pork well with salt and black pepper.

3. Add the oil to the pot, and move the pot around to spread evenly. Sear the pork in the oil. When you no longer see pink, turn the heat to low, and cook for 20 minutes, stirring occasionally. Add the chicken to the pot, and let cook for 10 minutes, stirring occasionally.

Remove the pork and chicken with a slotted spoon, and place in a bowl.

4. Add the sausage to the pot, and cook for 10 to 15 minutes or until you see some browning. Remove with a slotted spoon, reserving drippings in pot.

5. Add the yellow onion, bell pepper, green onion, celery, beef bouillon cubes, and Pi-YAHHHHH!! Seasoning to the pot. Sauté until completely soft, stirring occasionally, about 50 minutes.

6. At this point, preheat your oven to 300°.

7. Add the garlic to the vegetable mixture, and sauté for about 10 miinutes. Add the 3½ cups water, soup, hot sauce, and browning and seasoning sauce, and raise the heat. When the soup has blended, add the pasta and all meat back in. Mix well. Once everything is mixed nicely, gently press down on the top so that all pasta is touching liquid. Bring the mix to a boil. Once boiling, cover, turn the heat off, and put the pot in the oven.

8. Bake for exactly 1 hour. Do not touch that oven! Leave it alone! Trussme.

9. When done, remove the pot, and set aside for 5 minutes before uncovering. When the time is up, remove the cover, mix the top to the bottom, cover it back up, and let it sit for another 5 minutes. Garnish wth parsley, if desired, and then serve. Hope you enjoy!

TALES FROM THE BAYOU

There is a very funny secret behind this pastalaya. The first time I made it, I videoed it for Facebook and YouTube, and let's just say, it didn't go as smoothly as planned. This was in the very early stages of my page. At the time, pastalaya wasn't as common down here as it is now. Jambalaya always had more of a presence back then, but now, pastalaya seems to be served just as much at every festival and charitable event.

The day I decided to do this dish, I figured I would pretty much just follow my jambalaya recipe except I would finish it on the stove. As I was finishing, I kept having to cook it

longer. This turned into many segments of me filming myself opening the pot and then closing it and saying, "Cook it a little longer." It felt like I had no direction with this one. When the pasta was finally cooked to my liking, I knew I couldn't upload those clips. So, I videoed myself putting the pot in the oven, saying, "Cook for 1 hour at 300°," and then removing the pot saying it was done. I had no clue if this would work until people sent me their clips of it working perfectly. It was a risky move on my part, but it paid off. It works great, and it's a favorite amongst fans. I've since re-filmed it according to the directions, so don't worry.

SHRIMP & SAUSAGE PASTALAYA

MAKES 8 SERVINGS

1	tablespoon vegetable oil
1	pound smoked pork sausage, sliced
2	yellow onions, chopped
1	green bell pepper, chopped
1	bunch green onions, chopped
2	stalks celery, chopped
1	tablespoon minced garlic
½	tablespoon Pi-YAHHHHH!! Seasoning
3	chicken bouillon cubes
3½	cups water
1	(10.5-ounce) can cream of chicken soup
1	tablespoon hot sauce
1	tablespoon browning and seasoning sauce
1	(16-ounce) package bow tie pasta (or your favorite pasta)
1	pound peeled and deveined medium fresh shrimp

1. Start out by heating a pot over a medium heat.

2. Add the oil to the pot; add the sausage, and cook for about 10 minutes. Remove the sausage with a slotted spoon, and place in a bowl.

3. Add the yellow onion, bell pepper, green onion, celery, garlic, Pi-YAHHHHH!! Seasoning, and chicken bouillon cubes to the pot. Sauté until completely soft, about 1 hour. With about 5 minutes left of sautéing, add the 3½ cups water, soup, hot sauce, and browning and seasoning sauce, and raise the heat.

4. When the whole mixture has blended, add the sausage and pasta to the pot. Mix well. Once everything is mixed nicely, gently press down on the top so all pasta is touching liquid. Bring to a boil. Once boiling, cover, lower to a simmer, and let cook for 20 minutes.

5. Add the shrimp to the pot, and stir until combined; cover and cook for another 10 minutes. Remove the pot from heat, and set aside for 5 minutes before uncovering. Uncover, stir well, and serve. Hope you enjoy!

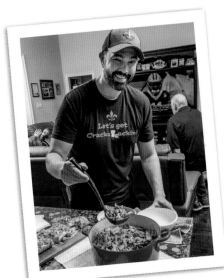

Pastalaya is great to feed a crowd. We like to cook up some on the weekends during football season.

BLACK BELT TIP

If you're worried about some of the pasta not being cooked all the way, after you stir the top to the bottom, just cover it back up and let it sit for another 5 minutes and then serve. Trussme.

CHICKEN & SAUSAGE PASTA

MAKES 6 SERVINGS

1 pound boneless chicken breast, cut into cubes

Salt and ground black pepper, to taste

1 tablespoon vegetable oil

1 pound smoked sausage, sliced

1 yellow onion, chopped

1 green bell pepper, chopped

1 red bell pepper, chopped

1 tablespoon minced garlic

1 (14.5-ounce) can chicken broth

1 quart half-and-half

1 tablespoon Pi-YAHHHHH!! Seasoning

1 tablespoon dried parsley

1 tablespoon hot sauce

1 (16-ounce) package penne pasta

1 cup shredded Parmesan cheese, plus more for sprinkling

1. Heat up a large pot over a medium-low heat.

2. Season the chicken with the salt and black pepper.

3. Add the oil to the pot. Drop in the sausage, and brown for 5 to 10 minutes. Remove the sausage from the pot, and place in a bowl off to the side.

4. Add the chicken to the pot, and cook for roughly 10 minutes. Remove the chicken.

5. Add the onion and bell peppers to the pot. Sauté for 20 minutes. Add the garlic, and continue sautéing for another 5 minutes. Add the chicken broth little by little, breaking up anything stuck to the bottom. Add the chicken and sausage, half-and-half, Pi-YAHHHHH!! Seasoning, parsley, and hot sauce. Raise the heat so it can come to a slight boil. When you begin to see a slight boil, add in the pasta. Mix into the pot so the pasta is covered by all the sauce. When it comes back to a boil, cover, lower to a simmer, and cook for 20 minutes. Uncover and mix well. Add the cheese. Once you see that the cheese is completely melted, turn the heat off, sprinkle with extra Parmesan, and serve!

BLACK BELT TIP

People ask me all the time what kind of sausage I recommend. The truth is, I'm not brand loyal when it comes to sausage. I like and use all different varieties and brands, so just use what you like best.

SPAGHETTI & MEATBALLS

MAKES 12 SERVINGS

Marinara:
½   cup olive oil
1   yellow onion, chopped
1   green bell pepper, chopped
2   stalks celery, chopped
1   (12-ounce) can tomato paste
1   tablespoon minced garlic
3   (15-ounce) cans tomato sauce
3   (14.5-ounce) cans diced tomatoes
2   (10-ounce) cans diced tomatoes with
     green chiles
¼   cup granulated sugar
1   tablespoon dried parsley
2   teaspoons salt
1   teaspoon dried basil
1   teaspoon ground black pepper
3   dried bay leaves
Dash crushed red pepper
1   cup water

Meatballs:
Olive oil, for coating
2   pounds ground chuck
2   slices white bread
1   cup Italian-seasoned bread crumbs
¾   cup grated Parmesan cheese, plus more
     for serving
3   large eggs, lightly beaten
1   teaspoon salt
1   teaspoon garlic powder
1   teaspoon ground black pepper
1   teaspoon dried basil
1   teaspoon dried oregano

Cooked spaghetti, to serve
Garnish: chopped fresh basil

1. For marinara: Start out by heating a large pot over a medium heat. Add the oil, onion, bell pepper, and celery, and cook down for 15 minutes. Add the tomato paste and garlic, and cook down for another 5 minutes, stirring frequently. Add the tomato sauce, diced tomatoes, and diced tomatoes with green chiles. Mix well. Add the sugar, parsley, salt, basil, black pepper, bay leaves, and crushed red pepper. Stir mixture well, and add 1 cup water. Raise heat until you start to see it bubble; lower heat to a simmer, and cover. Let simmer for 2 hours, stirring every 15 minutes.

2. For meatballs: Preheat your oven to 375°. Line a large pan with foil, and coat with oil.

3. Put your ground chuck in a large bowl.

4. Moisten your bread with some water, tear into small pieces, and add to your ground chuck. Add your bread crumbs, cheese, eggs, salt, garlic powder, black pepper, basil, and oregano. Mix well with your hands, and roll into golf ball-size balls. Gently place each meatball on your prepared pan.

5. Bake for 25 to 30 minutes. Gently add the meatballs to your sauce. Let simmer for at least another 30 minutes—the longer, the better. Serve with pasta and extra cheese. Garnish with fresh basil, if desired, and enjoy!

GROUND BEEF & SAUSAGE SPAGHETTI

MAKES 14 SERVINGS

1   pound Italian or green onion sausage
½   cup plus 1 tablespoon olive oil, divided
1   yellow onion, chopped
1   green bell pepper, chopped
2   stalks celery, chopped
2   pounds ground beef
½   tablespoon Pi-YAHHHHH!! Seasoning
½   tablespoon garlic powder
1   (12-ounce) can tomato paste
2   (10-ounce) cans diced tomatoes with
    green chiles
1   tablespoon minced garlic
2   (28-ounce) cans crushed tomatoes
3   (15-ounce) cans tomato sauce
¼   cup granulated sugar
1   tablespoon dried parsley
2   teaspoons salt
1   teaspoon dried basil
1   teaspoon ground black pepper
3   dried bay leaves
Dash crushed red pepper
2   cups water
Cooked spaghetti, to serve
Garlic bread, to serve
Garnish: chopped fresh basil

1. Start out by heating a large pot and a large pan over a medium heat. Also, preheat your oven to 375°.

2. Spray a baking sheet with cooking spray. Place your sausage on the prepared pan.

3. Bake for 1 hour.

4. Meanwhile, add ½ cup oil to your large pot; add the onion, bell pepper, and celery, and cook down for 10 minutes.

5. While your vegetables are sautéing, add the remaining 1 tablespoon oil to your pan, and start browning your ground beef. Season the beef with Pi-YAHHHHH!! Seasoning and garlic powder. Cook the beef until it's browned and crumbly; drain.

6. Add the tomato paste to the vegetable mixture, and cook down for another 10 minutes, stirring frequently. Add the diced tomatoes and minced garlic, and cook for another 5 minutes. Add the crushed tomatoes and tomato sauce. Add the sugar, parsley, salt, dried basil, black pepper, bay leaves, and red pepper. Add the ground beef and 2 cups water, and stir mixture well. Simmer until sausage is done baking.

7. When the sausage is done, let stand for 5 to 10 minutes to cool. Cut sausage into thirds or fourths, and add to the pot. Raise the heat until you start to see a slight boil; lower heat to a simmer, and cover. Let simmer for 2 hours, stirring every 15 minutes. Serve with pasta and garlic bread, and sprinkle with fresh basil, if desired. Enjoy!

TALES FROM THE BAYOU

To this day, I have never met a kinder person in my life than my grandmother Andra Oncale. I never once heard her speak negatively about anyone. She never even uttered a curse word. She was a special needs teacher who lived a simple life and gave whatever she could to her church and her community. She used to make this very simple ground meat spaghetti when I was a kid. I remember pretty much licking my plate clean. It's amazing how the simplest things impress us as children. In 2013, she passed away from Alzheimer's. I'm forever grateful to have had her guidance in my life.

CHICKEN SPAGHETTI

MAKES 14 SERVINGS

5 quarts water
2 (3- to 4-pound) whole chickens
2 yellow onions, divided
3 stalks celery, divided
2 carrots, peeled and cut into chunks
1 green bell pepper
2 tablespoons olive oil
1 tablespoon minced garlic
2 tablespoons plus 2 teaspoons salt, divided
1 tablespoon garlic powder
1 (12-ounce) can tomato paste
2 (10-ounce) cans diced tomatoes with green chiles
2 (28-ounce) cans crushed tomatoes
3 (15-ounce) cans tomato sauce
¼ cup granulated sugar
1 tablespoon dried parsley
1 teaspoon dried basil
1 teaspoon ground black pepper
Dash crushed red pepper
3 dried bay leaves
1 (16-ounce) package spaghetti
French bread, to serve
Garnish: chopped fresh parsley

1. Start out by heating a large pot over a medium heat.

2. Also, heat up a large stockpot filled with 5 quarts of water over a medium heat. Add the whole chickens to the stockpot.

3. Cut 1 onion and 1 stalk of celery into chunks; add them and the carrots to the stockpot with the chicken. Raise the heat to high and cover. As you start to see foam rise to the top, skim it out. Keep the lid on in between skimming; this will prevent too much water from evaporating.

4. Chop the bell pepper, remaining 1 onion, and remaining 1 stalk of celery.

5. Add the oil to the large pot. Add the chopped onion, chopped celery, chopped bell pepper, and minced garlic to the pot. Sauté for 25 minutes, stirring occasionally.

6. As the stockpot increases in heat and you've skimmed much of the foam, add 2 tablespoons salt and garlic powder. When the stockpot reaches a rolling boil, cover, lower to a simmer, and let cook for 1 hour.

7. Add the tomato paste to the vegetable mixture, and cook down for another 5 minutes. Add in the tomatoes with green chiles, and cook down for another 5 minutes. Mash down the tomatoes and vegetables with a slotted spatula or potato masher. Add the crushed tomatoes and tomato sauce. Add the sugar, parsley, basil, black pepper, crushed red pepper, bay leaves, and remaining 2 teaspoons salt. Blend everything together. Raise the heat so you start to see a slight boil. Be careful, as the sauce is thick and may pop. When you start to see some slight bubbling, cover the pot, lower to a simmer, and let cook for 2 hours, stirring the bottom every 10 minutes.

8. Meanwhile, your chicken stock should have finished cooking. Carefully remove the chicken, and place on a tray. Pour the remainder through a sieve over a large bowl or pot. You may have to do this a couple times so you can remove any lingering bits.

9. Once you have a clean broth, add 2 cups of broth to the sauce, and leave the remaining broth in a pot off to the side.

10. Let the chicken cool down for at least 1 hour. When the chicken is cool enough, you can go about pulling the meat off the bone.

11. After the sauce has cooked down for 2 hours, add the chicken, and let simmer for 1 hour.

12. With about 30 minutes left of cooking the sauce, heat up the remaining stock on a high heat. Once you've reached a rolling boil, add the pasta to the stock. Cook the pasta according to the package directions. Serve the pasta with the sauce and some French bread, garnish with fresh parsley, if desired, and enjoy!

BLACK BELT TIP

When people hear the name "chicken spaghetti," they often think of the cheesy, baked casserole. But this isn't that. This is Cajun Chicken Spaghetti with a slow-cooked tomato sauce and tender chicken. It's a fan-favorite in my house. My wife, Misty, especially loves it. It takes some time, but it's worth it. Let's get crackalackin'!

FOUR-CHEESE LASAGNA

MAKES 8 SERVINGS

¼ cup plus 1 tablespoon olive oil, divided
1 yellow onion, chopped
1 green bell pepper, chopped
2 stalks celery, chopped
1 (12-ounce) can tomato paste
2 (10-ounce) cans mild diced tomatoes with green chiles
1 tablespoon minced garlic
2 (28-ounces) cans crushed tomatoes
3 (15-ounce) cans tomato sauce
¼ cup granulated sugar
1 tablespoon dried parsley
3 teaspoons salt, divided
2 teaspoons ground black pepper, divided
1 teaspoon dried basil
Dash crushed red pepper
3 dried bay leaves
2 cups water
1 pound ground beef
1 pound hot blend breakfast sausage
1 teaspoon Pi-YAHHHHH!! Seasoning
1 teaspoon garlic powder
1 stick salted butter
½ cup all-purpose flour
4 cups warm whole milk
1 (16-ounce) package lasagna noodles (see Black Belt Tip)
½ cup grated Parmesan cheese
1 (8-ounce) block provolone cheese, shredded
1 (8-ounce) block Havarti cheese, shredded
1 (8-ounce) block mozzarella cheese, shredded
Garnish: chopped fresh basil

1. Start out by heating a large pot over a medium heat.

2. Add the ¼ cup oil to the pot. Add the onion, bell pepper, and celery. Sauté for 10 minutes. Add in the tomato paste. Sauté for another 10 minutes. Add in the diced tomatoes and minced garlic. Sauté for another 5 minutes. Toward the end of sautéing, use a large fork to smash the tomatoes. Add the crushed tomatoes, tomato sauce, sugar, parsley, 2 teaspoons salt, 1 teaspoon black pepper, basil, crushed red pepper, and bay leaves, and blend evenly.

3. Add the 2 cups water to the tomato cans so you can get up any tomato or sauce left in the cans, and pour into the pot. Raise your heat to where you see a slight boil; cover, lower to a simmer, and let cook for 2 hours, stirring every 20 minutes.

4. At about the 1-hour mark, start heating a large pan over a medium heat off to the side.

5. Preheat the oven to 350°.

6. Add the remaining 1 tablespoon oil to the pan; add ground beef and sausage. Season the meat with the Pi-YAHHHHH!! Seasoning and garlic powder, and cook until browned and crumbly; drain, and set off to the side. Wipe down your pan really good.

7. Put the pan over a low heat. Add the butter to the pan. Once the butter has melted, blend in the flour. Continue blending until you have a smooth blond or tan color roux. Once you've reached a blond roux, blend in the warm milk a little at a time. After all the milk has been added and you have a creamy white gravy, add the remaining 1 teaspoon salt and remaining 1 teaspoon black pepper, and blend evenly.

8. If you're at the 2-hour mark of your sauce, turn all your heat off and begin fixing the lasagna. In an 11x8-inch baking dish, you will add a bottom layer of tomato sauce, a layer of raw lasagna noodles, another generous layer of tomato sauce, a layer of beef mixture, three rows of white gravy over the beef, Parmesan, and the provolone. For the next layer, repeat the same process, starting with raw noodles and continuing with layers of tomato sauce, beef mixture, and white gravy. Sprinkle with Havarti. For the third layer, repeat the same process with layers of raw noodles, tomato sauce, beef mixture, and white gravy. Top with mozzarella. Cover with foil.

9. Bake for 30 minutes. Remove the foil, increase the oven temperature to 375°, and bake for another 30 minutes. When done, let stand for 10 minutes, and garnish with basil, if desired. Use a knife and spatula to cut the first piece, and enjoy!

BLACK BELT TIP

You may not need to use the entire package of lasagna noodles. You may also have some leftover meat, tomato sauce, and white gravy. Save any remaining ingredients for another recipe.

CRAWFISH LASAGNA

MAKES 8 SERVINGS

½   stick salted butter
1   yellow onion, chopped
1   green bell pepper, chopped
2   stalks celery, chopped
1   (8-ounce) package cremini mushrooms, finely chopped
1   (10-ounce) can diced tomatoes with green chiles
2   pounds crawfish tails
1   tablespoon minced garlic
½   tablespoon Pi-YAHHHHH!! Seasoning
Salt, to taste
1   (16-ounce) package lasagna noodles
1   (8-ounce) package cream cheese, softened
½   cup grated Parmesan cheese
2   (10.5-ounce) cans cream of mushroom soup
1   tablespoon chopped fresh parsley
½   tablespoon dried basil
1   (8-ounce) block jalapeño Havarti cheese, shredded
1   (8-ounce) block mozzarella cheese, shredded
Garnish: fresh parsley

1. Start out by heating a large pan over a medium-low heat.

2. Melt the butter in the large pan. Once the butter has completely melted, drop in the onion, bell pepper, and celery. Let simmer for roughly 10 minutes, stirring occasionally. Add the chopped mushrooms, and sauté for another 10 minutes. Add the tomatoes, and sauté for another 10 minutes. Add the crawfish tails, minced garlic, and the Pi-YAHHHHH!! Seasoning. Sauté for 10 minutes.

3. At this time, bring a large pot of water to a boil. Once the water has been brought to a boil, season the water with salt, and add the lasagna noodles; cook for 9 minutes. Drain, reserving some of the pasta water. (If the pasta tends to bind together, the pasta water can help break it apart while maintaining good pasta starch.)

4. After the 10 minutes of sautéing is up, add the cream cheese to the crawfish mixture, and blend until completely melted. Add the Parmesan, and blend evenly. Turn the heat off, and let stand.

5. In a large bowl, combine the soup, parsley, and basil.

6. Preheat your oven to 350°.

7. Spray the bottom of a 13x9-inch baking dish with cooking spray.

8. In the pan with crawfish mixture, move the mixture to one side of the pan. Lean the pan so that the liquid sauce moves to the other side of the pan. Use this sauce to layer the bottom of the baking dish. Add one-third of lasagna noodles. Add one-third of the soup mixture. Add one-third of the crawfish mixture. Add one-third of Harvarti and mozzarella. Starting with noodles, repeat layers twice.

9. Bake for 30 to 40 minutes or until the inner sides of the dish are bubbling. Let cool for 10 minutes when done. Garnish with fresh parsley, if desired, and enjoy!

This is our golden retriever, Dash, just a few days after we got him.

SEAFOOD LASAGNA

MAKES 8 SERVINGS

½   stick salted butter
1   yellow onion, chopped
1   green bell pepper, chopped
2   stalks celery, chopped
1   (10-ounce) can diced tomatoes with green chiles
1   tablespoon minced garlic
2   teaspoons salt, divided
1   (16-ounce) package lasagna noodles
1   (8-ounce) package cream cheese, softened
½   cup grated Parmesan cheese
1   pound crawfish tails
1   pound peeled and deveined small fresh shrimp
½   tablespoon Pi-YAHHHHH!! Seasoning
½   stick unsalted butter
¼   cup all-purpose flour
1   pint half-and-half
1   teaspoon ground black pepper
1   tablespoon chopped fresh parsley
½   tablespoon dried basil
1   pound lump crabmeat, picked free of shell
1   (8-ounce) block mozzarella cheese, shredded
1   (8-ounce) block jalapeño Havarti cheese, shredded

1. Start out by heating a large pan over a medium-low heat.

2. Melt the salted butter in the large pan. Once the butter has completely melted, drop in the onion, bell pepper, and celery. Let simmer for roughly 20 minutes, stirring occasionally.

3. At this time, bring a large pot of water to a boil.

4. Add the tomatoes and garlic to your vegetable mixture, and sauté for another 10 minutes.

5. When water has reached a boil, season the water with 1 teaspoon salt, and add the lasagna noodles; cook for 9 minutes. Drain, reserving some of the pasta water. (If the pasta is stuck together, the pasta water can help break it apart while maintaining good pasta starch.)

6. At this time, begin to get a small pot or pan heated over a low heat.

7. Add the cream cheese to the vegetable mixture, and blend until completely melted. Add the Parmesan, and blend evenly. Add the crawfish, shrimp, and Pi-YAHHHHH!! Seasoning. Sauté for 10 minutes or until the shrimp have firmed up, turning a light pink color. Once reached, turn the heat off, and let stand.

8. Meanwhile, in the small pan, melt the unsalted butter. Add the flour, and begin stirring quickly until you reach a smooth blond roux. Add a small amount of the half-and-half. Continue stirring as you add more. Once you've added in all the half-and-half and you've reached a white gravy, add in the black pepper and remaining 1 teaspoon salt. Add the parsley and basil, and mix well. Turn the heat off, and set aside.

9. Preheat your oven to 350°.

10. Spray the bottom of a 13x9-inch baking dish with cooking spray.

11. In the pan with the crawfish mixture, move the mixture to one side of the pan. Lean the pan so the liquid sauce moves to the other side of the pan. Use this sauce to layer the bottom of the baking dish. Add one-third of noodles. Add one-third of the bechamel. Add one-third of crawfish mixture. Add one-third of crabmeat. Add one-third of mozzarella and Havarti. Starting with noodles, repeat layers twice.

12. Bake for 40 to 45 minutes or until you start to see a golden color form around the edges. Let cool for 10 minutes when done. Enjoy!

CHICKEN FAJITA PASTA

MAKES 8 SERVINGS

2 to 3 pounds boneless chicken breast, cut
    into bite-size pieces
1   tablespoon Pi-YAHHHHH!! Seasoning
1   tablespoon vegetable oil
1   yellow onion, sliced
1   green bell pepper, sliced into strips
1   red bell pepper, sliced into strips
Cold water, if needed
1   (14.5-ounce) can chicken broth
1   tablespoon chili powder
2   teaspoons ground cumin
1   teaspoon garlic powder
3   cups whole milk
½   teaspoon salt
1   (16-ounce) package penne
1   (8-ounce) block jalapeño Havarti cheese,
    shredded

1. Start out by heating a large pan over a medium heat.

2. Season the chicken with the Pi-YAHHHHH!! Seasoning, and set aside.

3. Add the oil to the pan. Drop in the chicken. Sear the chicken for 8 to 10 minutes. Remove the chicken from the pan, and place in a bowl to the side.

4. Add the onion and bell peppers to the pan. Sauté for about 30 minutes. (In the middle of the 30 minutes of sautéing, if you start to see too much browning on the bottom of the pan, just add a small amount of cold water to break it up.)

5. Add a small amount of the chicken broth to the vegetable mixture to break up the bottom. Add the rest of the chicken broth. Add the chili powder, cumin, and garlic powder. Add the chicken back to the pan. Raise the heat to high so it comes to a slight boil. Once you've reached a slight boil, cover, lower to a simmer, and let it cook for 30 minutes.

6. Add the milk and salt to the pan. Add the pasta, and mix around so all the pasta is in the liquid. Raise the heat back to high. When you've reached a boil, cover, lower to a simmer, and cook for 20 minutes. Stir, and add the cheese. Mix well. Once the cheese has completely melted, turn your heat off. Serve, and enjoy!

Matt Schnell is a professional mixed martial artist from Louisiana whom I have been following for more than 10 years. He started out on the small circuit, and ended up landing a spot on MTV's reality show Caged. *After humble beginnings, he eventually fought his way into the UFC.*

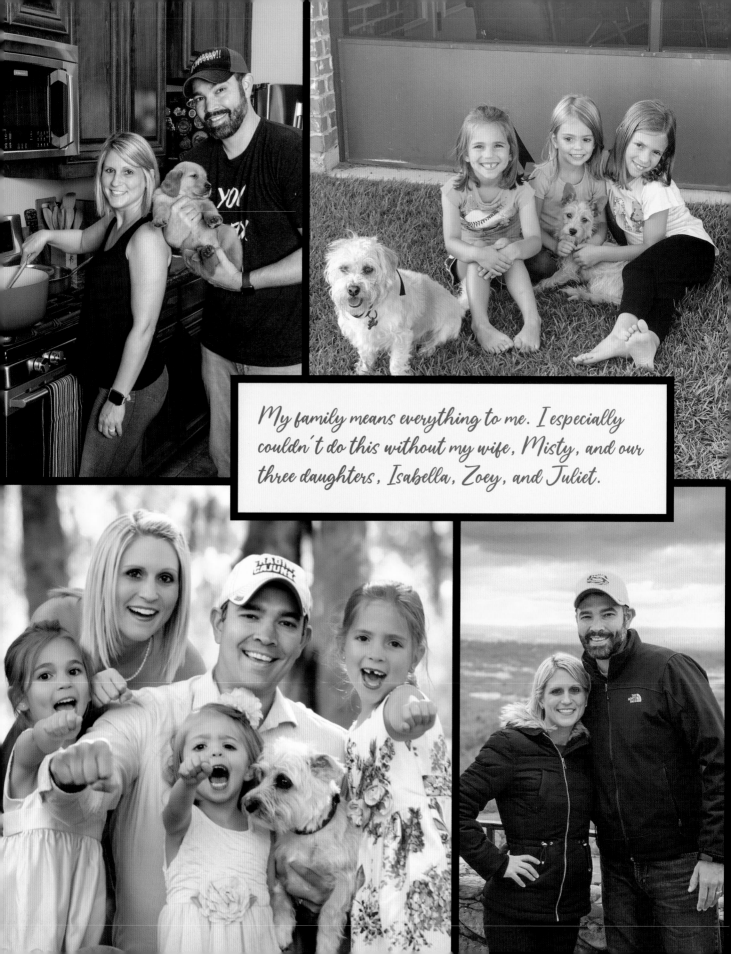

My family means everything to me. I especially couldn't do this without my wife, Misty, and our three daughters, Isabella, Zoey, and Juliet.

6 | *YOU DEUX YOU DINNERS*
BEEF, PORK, AND CHICKEN FEASTS

SMOTHERED PORK CHOPS & ONION GRAVY

MAKES 6 TO 8 SERVINGS

6 to 8 bone-in pork chops
1 teaspoon Pi-YAHHHHH!! Seasoning, plus more to season meat
1 tablespoon vegetable oil
2 yellow onions, chopped
1 stick unsalted butter
⅓ cup all-purpose flour
1 (32-ounce) container chicken stock
2 tablespoons cornstarch
2 tablespoons cold water
Hot cooked rice or mashed potatoes, and corn, to serve
Garnish: chopped fresh parsley

1. Start out by heating a pan over a medium-high heat.

2. Generously season each side of the pork chops with Pi-YAHHHHH!! Seasoning.

3. Add oil to the hot pan. In batches, add the pork chops, and sear them for 5 to 6 minutes on each side. When you remove them, you want to put them on a plate or in a bowl to help save any excess liquid that comes off them.

4. Add the onions to the pan. Let the onions cover all the drippings on the bottom of the pan for about 30 seconds and then begin stirring. The steam from the onions will help break up the drippings on the bottom of the pan. Feel free to add a small amount of cold water and scrape with a wooden spoon to further help break up any drippings. Sauté the onions for 5 minutes and then add the butter. Once the butter is melted, add the flour, and stir to combine. Cook down, stirring frequently, for another 25 to 30 minutes or until you see some nice browning forming.

5. When your onions are soft and brown, add a small amount of chicken stock, and mix well. You want to get a creamy consistency. Add most of the remaining chicken stock to the pan. Layer your pork chops over the onion gravy. Be sure to pour any liquid from the plate of pork chops back into the pan as well. Add Pi-YAHHHHH!! Seasoning and any remaining chicken stock. Bring to a boil; cover and lower to a simmer. Cook for 2 hours. Feel free to gently stir every 15 minutes.

6. After 2 hours, mix the cornstarch and 2 tablespoons cold water together. Stir the cornstarch mixture into the gravy. Serve with either rice or mashed potatoes, and corn. Garnish with parsley, if desired.

TALES FROM THE BAYOU

My mom is a registered nurse who worked a lot of night shifts when I was growing up. My dad loved to watch cooking shows on television, but he wasn't much of a cook. Needless to say, we weren't one of those families that sat down to homecooked meals every night of the week. But when my mom did cook, one of my favorite meals was her smothered pork chops. The pork chops got so tender and there was always lots of gravy that soaked into the rice. It's hard to beat a meal cooked by your mom, but maybe this dish will become a favorite in your home, too.

This is my mom and dad.

CABBAGE ROLLS

MAKES 6 TO 8 SERVINGS

Sauce:
2   tablespoons olive oil
1   yellow onion, chopped
1   green bell pepper, chopped
1   stalk celery, chopped
1   tablespoon minced garlic
1   (6-ounce) can tomato paste
1   (28-ounce) can crushed tomatoes
1   (15-ounce) can tomato sauce
1   (8-ounce) can tomato sauce
1½ tablespoons granulated sugar
½   tablespoon dried parsley
1   teaspoon salt
½   teaspoon dried basil
¼   teaspoon black pepper
Dash crushed red pepper
2   dried bay leaves

Rolls:
1   large head cabbage
1¼ cups long-grain rice
1   tablespoon olive oil
1   bunch green onions, chopped
1   yellow onion, chopped
2   stalks celery, chopped
1   tablespoon minced garlic
1   pound ground beef
1   pound hot breakfast sausage
1   tablespoon dried parsley
1   tablespoon Pi-YAHHHHH!! Seasoning
1   tablespoon Worcestershire sauce
½   cup plain bread crumbs
1   large egg

1. For the sauce: In a large pot over medium heat, add oil; add yellow onion, bell pepper, and celery. Sauté for about 10 minutes. Add garlic. Sauté for 5 minutes more.

2. Add tomato paste, and cook for 5 minutes more. Add crushed tomatoes, both cans of tomato sauce, sugar, parsley, salt, basil, black pepper, crushed red pepper, and bay leaves. Bring to a slight boil. Cover, reduce heat to a simmer, and cook for 2 hours, stirring every 10 minutes so sauce doesn't stick to bottom of pot. After 2 hours, remove pot from heat, and set aside.

3. For the rolls: Cut cabbage to remove hard center stem. Cut inward, about 2 inches away from hard stem, all the way around the cabbage; discard stem.

4. Bring a large pot of water to a boil over a high heat. Add cabbage, cut side downward, and boil for 10 minutes. Remove from pot; set aside.

5. Cook rice according to package directions; set aside.

6. In a large pot over a medium heat, add oil; add green onion, yellow onion, and celery. Sauté for about 10 minutes. Add garlic. Sauté for 5 minutes more. Add ground beef, breakfast sausage, parsley, Pi-YAHHHHH!! Seasoning, and Worcestershire sauce. Cook for 5 minutes more. Turn heat off, and transfer filling to a non-metal bowl.

7. Carefully remove leaves individually from cabbage. Carefully trim side of the stem so it's flush with the rest of the leaf.

8. Combine filling, cooked rice, bread crumbs, and egg.

9. Preheat the oven to 375°.

10. In a 13x9-inch baking dish, spoon a layer of the sauce.

11. In a cabbage leaf, place a large scoop of filling in center. Wrap egg roll style; fold backside over the top of filling, tucking in sides and continuing to roll. Place seam side down in baking dish. You may need to adjust each roll so that all of them can fit in the dish. Once you have all the rolls in the dish, cover with sauce. Loosely cover with foil.

12. Bake for 1½ hours. Let cool for 10 minutes. Serve, and enjoy!

RED BEANS & SAUSAGE

MAKES 6 TO 8 SERVINGS

1	pound smoked sausage, divided
1	tablespoon oil
½	pound smoked tasso, sliced
1	yellow onion, chopped
1	green bell pepper, chopped
3	stalks celery, chopped
1	tablespoon minced garlic
7	cups water, divided
1	(32-ounce) container chicken broth
1	pound dried red kidney beans
1	tablespoon Pi-YAHHHHH!! Seasoning
1	tablespoon dried parsley
1	teaspoon salt
2	dried bay leaves
Hot cooked rice, to serve

1. Start out by heating a large pot over a medium heat.

2. Slice half of smoked sausage crosswise and leave the remainder of the sausage whole.

3. Add oil to pot. Drop in the sliced and whole sausage and tasso. Sear until you see a slight browning form on the meat, 5 to

10 minutes. Remove the meat from the pot, and place in a bowl off to the side.

4. Add the onion, bell pepper, and celery to the pot, and slowly work the bottom. Try to get up all remaining drippings. Sauté for 25 to 30 minutes. When you have about 5 minutes left of sautéing, add the garlic.

5. Meanwhile, in a medium pot, add 5 cups water and the chicken broth. Heat over a high heat.

6. Rinse the beans in a colander, and add the beans to the pot of liquid. Once the pot has reached a rolling boil, let boil, uncovered, for 10 minutes. After the 10-minute mark, turn the heat off.

7. Once you've sautéed the vegetables for 25 to 30 minutes, add the beans and liquid to the large pot. Add the remaining 2 cups water. Add the Pi-YAHHHHH!! Seasoning, parsley, salt, and bay leaves. Bring to a boil; cover and lower heat to a simmer. Let simmer for 3 hours, stirring the bottom every 10 to 15 minutes.

8. After the three-hour mark, uncover, and check the consistency of the beans. For a thicker consistency, remove a few large spoonfuls of beans, and place in a bowl on the side. Mash the beans in the bowl into a creamy mixture. Add the creamy mixture back to the pot. Continue this method until you reach your desired consistency. Add the sliced and whole sausage and tasso back into the pot and continue to simmer just until sausage and tasso are heated through. Ladle a serving over a bed of rice, and enjoy!

Misty is almost always in the kitchen helping me.

STUFFED BELL PEPPERS

MAKES 6 SERVINGS

1 tablespoon olive oil
1 pound ground beef
1 yellow onion, chopped
2 stalks celery, chopped
1 (10.5-ounce) can cream of mushroom soup
½ tablespoon Pi-YAHHHHH!! Seasoning
½ teaspoon garlic salt
½ teaspoon cayenne pepper
½ teaspoon ground black pepper
6 assorted bell peppers
4 cups water
1½ cups long-grain rice
1 tablespoon plus 1 teaspoon salt, divided
6 tablespoons seasoned bread crumbs
6 tablespoons salted butter

1. Start out by heating a pot over a medium-low heat.

2. Add the oil to the pot. Brown the ground beef in the pot, and drain out the excess fat. Remove the beef.

3. Add the onion and celery to the pot. Sauté for about 15 minutes. Add the ground beef back in. Sauté for another 5 minutes. Add the soup. Fill the soup can halfway with water, breaking up any remaining soup. Pour into the pot. Add the Pi-YAHHHHH!! Seasoning, garlic salt, cayenne, and black pepper. Cover and simmer for about 1½ hours, stirring every 15 minutes.

4. Begin heating a large pot of water over a high heat.

5. Meanwhile, cut the tops off the bell peppers, and clean out all the remnants on the inside. Be sure to take your knife along the inside wall to remove any white membrane.

6. At this time, combine 4 cups water, rice, and 1 teaspoon salt in a medium pot, and bring to a boil. Cover and lower to a simmer. Simmer for 25 minutes. After 25 minutes is up, remove from heat, and let sit for 5 minutes before uncovering.

7. Once the large pot of water has reached a boil, add remaining 1 tablespoon salt, and drop in the bell peppers. Cook until you begin to see the bell peppers change to a lighter color, 10 to 15 minutes. Remove the bell peppers, and place in a bowl filled with ice water off to the side.

8. At this time, preheat your oven to 350°.

9. Once the bell peppers have cooled off, move them to a baking sheet covered with paper towels. Place them cut side down so any excess water can drain out of them.

10. When the beef mixture is done cooking, turn the heat off, and add the cooked rice. Mix well. Stuff each individual bell pepper with the beef and rice mixture; top each with 1 tablespoon bread crumbs and 1 tablespoon butter.

11. Bake for 25 minutes. Let cool for 5 to 10 minutes, and enjoy!

SMOTHERED BURRITOS

MAKES 4 TO 6 SERVINGS

1 teaspoon vegetable oil
2 pounds ground beef
2 yellow onions, chopped
Cold water, if needed
1 tablespoon minced garlic
1 (10-ounce) can diced tomatoes with green chiles
1 (15-ounce) can Ranch Style Beans
1 tablespoon chili powder
1 (1-ounce) package taco seasoning mix
1 (1-ounce) package ranch seasoning mix
1 teaspoon garlic powder
Sour cream
8 large flour tortillas
1 (10-ounce) can enchilada sauce
1 (8-ounce) block jalapeño Havarti cheese, shredded
Optional toppings: lettuce, tomato, avocado, jalapeño, onions, sour cream

1. Start out by heating a large pot over a medium-low heat.

2. Add oil to the hot pot, coating the bottom of the pot evenly. Add the ground beef. Cook until the beef is browned and crumbly. Remove the beef from the pot, and place in a sieve set over a plate of paper towels to catch excess fat.

3. Add the onion to the pot. Cook the onion for 25 to 30 minutes or until soft. If there are times you see a lot of browning forming on the bottom of the pot, feel free to add a small amount of cold water to help break things up. With about 5 minutes left of sautéing, add the minced garlic. Add the diced tomatoes. Use the liquid from the can of diced tomatoes to help break things up on the bottom of the pot. Add the cooked ground beef and Ranch Style Beans. Add the chili powder, taco seasoning, ranch seasoning, and garlic powder. Blend evenly. Cover and cook over a low heat for 1 hour, stirring every 5 minutes or so to break up anything sticking to the bottom.

4. Preheat your oven to 325°.

5. Remove the pot from the heat.

6. Spray a 13x9-inch baking dish with cooking spray.

7. Spread a dollop of sour cream along the top side of a flour tortilla. Place a large spoonful of the filling on the tortilla. Wrap by folding over the sides about 1 inch inward and then folding over the bottom toward the top, rolling over until the sour cream part sticks as the bottom seam. Repeat the process until all burritos are wrapped. Place in prepared pan. Add a spoonful of the enchilada sauce on the top of each burrito. Spread evenly. Sprinkle the cheese across the top.

8. Bake, uncovered, for 30 minutes. Let cool for 10 minutes. Serve with desired toppings, and enjoy!

BLACK BELT TIP

You may think sautéing the onion for 30 minutes is excessive, but cooking it low and slow gives it great flavor, and that's what these burritos are all about. Between the caramelized onions, seasonings, Ranch Style Beans, and spicy cheese, there's no lack of flavor. The sour cream smeared onto the tortilla helps seal the burritos up.

MEATY JAMBALAYA

MAKES 8 SERVINGS

1   **pound pork roast, cubed**
1   **pound boneless skinless chicken thighs, cubed**
Kosher salt and ground black pepper, to taste
1   **tablespoon vegetable oil**
1   **pound smoked sausage, sliced**
2   **yellow onions, chopped**
1   **green bell pepper, chopped**
1   **bunch green onions, chopped**
2   **stalks celery, chopped**
Cold water, as needed
3   **beef bouillon cubes**
1   **tablespoon minced garlic**
½   **tablespoon Pi-YAHHHHH!! Seasoning**
1   **teaspoon salt**
3½   **cups water**
2   **cups long-grain rice**
1   **tablespoon hot sauce**
1   **tablespoon browning and seasoning sauce**

1. First, start out by heating an oven-safe pot over a medium heat.

2. Season the pork and chicken well with kosher salt and black pepper.

3. Add the oil to the pot; add the pork, and sear for 20 minutes. Add the chicken, and cook for another 10 minutes, stirring occasionally. Remove the chicken and pork from the pot.

4. Add the sausage to the pot, and brown for 10 minutes.

5. At this point, preheat your oven to 300°.

6. Remove the sausage from the pot, reserving the drippings in the pot. Add the yellow onion, bell pepper, green onion, and celery to the drippings, and sauté for roughly 50 minutes. If you see too much browning forming on the bottom of the pot, just add a small amount of cold water to break things up.

7. Add the beef bouillon cubes, garlic, Pi-YAHHHHH!! Seasoning, and salt to the vegetable mixture. Sauté for another 10 minutes. Add the meats, 3½ cups water, rice, hot sauce, and browning and seasoning sauce, and stir. Bring to a boil; once boiling, cover.

8. Bake for exactly 1 hour. Remember, do not touch that oven! Leave it alone! Trust me. Once done, remove the jambalaya, and set aside for 5 minutes. Do not uncover until time is up! When the time is up, remove the cover, mix everything well, and serve. Hope you enjoy!

TALES FROM THE BAYOU

Martial arts is a big part of our family. My dad first introduced me to it when I was a kid, and I've loved it ever since. In 2021, I earned my fourth degree black belt in Taekwondo, officially making me a Master in the art. The day this photo was taken, all of my girls tested for a new rank at the same time. This was the first time for that to ever happen. Even Misty was in Taekwondo during this time and tested for her yellow belt. Shortly after, life happened, and Misty was unable to come to class. Since then, they've all tested separately, but this one photo will always be special to me. Having a hobby the whole family enjoys means a lot to me.

FRIED TURKEY & TURKEY GRAVY

MAKES 6 TO 8 SERVINGS

Turkey:
1   (12- to 15-pound) frozen whole turkey, thawed
8   ounces Cajun or Creole injector marinade
Pi-YAHHHHH!! Seasoning, to taste
3 to 4 gallons frying oil (preferably peanut oil)

Gravy:
8   cups water
2   carrots, cut into large pieces
2   stalks celery, cut into large pieces
1   yellow onion, cut into large pieces
4   cloves garlic
Turkey neck
Turkey liver
Turkey gizzard
½   tablespoon Pi-YAHHHHH!! Seasoning
1   teaspoon salt, plus more to taste
1   stick salted butter
½   cup all-purpose flour
Ground black pepper, to taste

1. For turkey: Make sure your turkey is fully defrosted. Remove, reserve, and refrigerate turkey neck, liver, and gizzard for gravy. The night before frying, inject the marinade in various spots on the turkey. Season the turkey generously with Pi-YAHHHHH!! Seasoning, and refrigerate overnight.

2. When ready to start frying, fill a tall 7- to 8-gallon pot with 3 gallons of frying oil. Using a propane burner placed outdoors and away from your house, heat the pot over a medium-high heat, and gradually get to 350°.

3. For gravy: While the oil is heating up, back in the house, heat a medium pot with 8 cups water over a high heat.

4. Add carrots, celery, onion, and garlic to the pot of water. Add the reserved turkey neck, liver, and gizzard, and Pi-YAHHHHH!! Seasoning and salt. Once the pot has reached a boil, cover, lower to a simmer, and cook

for 1 hour. When the hour is up, drain through a sieve over a large bowl so only a clean stock remains.

5. When the frying oil has reached 350°, slowly—and I mean *slowly*—lower the turkey into the pot. You may even have to hold it for a bit before you lower the entire way. Lowering too fast can cause a huge overspill and, in some cases, a fire. So, please, lower slowly.

6. Once the turkey is completely submerged, you set a timer for 3½ minutes per pound. For example, you'd cook a 12-pound turkey for about 42 minutes. Set a timer for a couple minutes before done so you are standing ready when it is done. Make sure you have someone keep watch of the turkey while you go inside to make the gravy.

7. While the turkey is frying, heat a medium pot over a medium-low heat on the stove.

8. Melt the stick of butter in the pot. Add the flour, and stir frequently until you reach a caramel color. This may take about 45 minutes. If the turkey finishes before the roux, just turn the heat off, and return when you're done removing the turkey.

9. When removing the turkey, let it hang over the pot for a bit so that much of the oil can drain from the turkey. Set the turkey down on a tray, and bring inside.

10. Finish getting the roux to a caramel color and then slowly start to add ladles of the stock to the roux. Keep adding and stirring until you reach your desired consistency. Season with salt and pepper if you find it needs more.

11. Once you have your gravy done, carve up and serve. Enjoy!

BLACK BELT TIP

We've all seen those videos that surface every Thanksgiving of fried turkeys gone wrong. These are a few ground rules to avoid any mishaps.
1. Make sure your turkey is completely thawed.
2. Always fry your turkey outside.
3. Lower your turkey into the oil VERY slowly.

MEAT PIES

MAKES 25

Filling:
2   tablespoons olive oil, divided
1   pound ground beef
1   yellow onion, chopped
1   small green bell pepper, chopped
1   stalk celery, chopped
1   tablespoon minced garlic
1   (10.5-ounce) can cream of chicken soup
½   tablespoon Pi-YAHHHHH!! Seasoning
1   teaspoon garlic salt

Pastry:
2   cups all-purpose flour
½   teaspoon cayenne pepper
1   (8-ounce) package cream cheese, cubed
1   stick salted butter, cubed
1   large egg

Vegetable oil, for frying
Garnish: chopped fresh parsley

1. For the filling: Start out by getting a pot heated over a medium heat.

2. Add 1 tablespoon olive oil to hot pot; add ground beef, and cook until browned. Strain through a sieve.

3. Add the remaining 1 tablespoon olive oil to the pot; drop the onion, bell pepper, and celery in, and sauté for 20 minutes. Add the minced garlic, and sauté for another 5 minutes. Add the ground beef and the soup. Feel free to add a small amount of water to the can so you can get any excess soup. Add the Pi-YAHHHHH!! Seasoning and garlic salt. Lower heat to a simmer, and cover. Simmer for 1 hour, stirring every 15 minutes.

4. For the pastry: Mix the flour and cayenne first so it blends well. Then add the cream cheese, butter, and egg. Knead the dough with your hands or a mixer for 5 minutes. Form into a ball, wrap tight with plastic wrap, and refrigerate for at least 30 minutes.

5. Once your filling has been simmering for at least 1 hour, move the pot to the freezer, and let chill for 30 minutes.

6. Roll dough to a ¼-inch thickness. Cut using a 3¾-inch round cutter. Place 2 teaspoons filling in center of each round. Fold dough over, and crimp with a fork. Finish with remaining filling. May have to reroll a few times. Place in refrigerator until ready to fry.

7. At this time, you can get a frying pan with about 1½ inches of vegetable oil heated over medium heat. You can test the readiness of your oil by dropping a small piece of pastry in there to see if it sizzles.

8. Once you have made all the pies, begin frying. Fry on one side until you start to see golden color form on the edges and then turn. When the pies have a good golden color on all sides, remove from oil, and set aside on a tray layered with paper towels. Let cool for 5 minutes, garnish with parsley, if desired, and enjoy!

TALES FROM THE BAYOU

I always feel so much nostalgia when I eat a meat pie. In middle school, they were one of those items that were served every so often at lunch. If you were lucky, you got to sit by the one kid who didn't like them and you traded your dessert for an extra one. Some of my fondest memories growing up were Sundays when we were headed to church. My mom would stop at this gas station in Bayou Blue where I would have a meat pie and a cream soda for breakfast. I know that seems odd for breakfast, but gas station food is often a traditional Cajun breakfast. Honestly, some of the best food you'll ever eat is probably around the corner at local gas stations in south Louisiana.

ROAST BEEF PO' BOYS

MAKES 6

2 tablespoons vegetable oil
1 (3-pound) Angus chuck roast
Pi-YAHHHHH!! Seasoning, to taste
All-purpose flour, for dusting
1 yellow onion, chopped
Cold water, as needed
1 cup water
1 (2-ounce) package onion soup mix
1 tablespoon Worcestershire sauce
1 tablespoon Pickapeppa Sauce
1 tablespoon minced garlic
¼ cup cold water
2 tablespoons cornstarch
Salted butter, softened
6 po' boy buns
Mayonnaise, lettuce, tomatoes, and pickles, to serve

1. Coat the bottom of a Dutch oven with the oil; place pot over a medium heat.

2. Generously season both sides of roast with Pi-YAHHHHH!! Seasoning. Dust all sides of the roast with a light coat of flour.

3. Add the roast to the pot, and sear for 6 to 8 minutes on each side. Remove from pot, and place in a bowl; set aside.

4. Add onion to the pot. Stir to break up drippings. If things really seem to be sticking to the bottom, then add a small amount of cold water to help break things up. Sauté for 20 minutes.

5. Meanwhile, mix 1 cup water, onion soup mix, Worcestershire sauce, and Pickapeppa Sauce in a medium bowl.

6. Add garlic to the pot, and sauté for another 5 to 10 minutes. Add a small amount of soup mixture. Stir to break up any remaining drippings stuck to the bottom. Return roast to pot, and pour remaining soup mixture on top of roast. Increase heat to high, and bring to a boil. Cover, reduce heat to a simmer, and let cook for 2 hours, turning the roast halfway through cooking so the other side cooks down in the liquid. After the 2-hour mark, carefully remove roast, and place in a bowl; set aside.

7. Mix the ¼ cup cold water and cornstarch in a bowl. Add cornstarch mixture to pot of gravy by pouring and stirring at the same time.

8. Shred roast, and return it to pot. Simmer for 30 minutes more, stirring every 5 minutes.

9. Just before serving, spread butter on po' boy buns, and place butter side down in a large skillet or griddle over a medium-high heat until golden brown. Remove from heat, and dress your po' boy how you like. Enjoy!

TALES FROM THE BAYOU

Folks from Louisiana aren't ones to hold back on sharing their opinions, and one subject that gets them fired up is the kind of bread used to make a po' boy. In the Bayou State, many po' boys are served on French bread. Louisianans especially love the bread from a bakery in New Orleans called Leidenheimer Baking Company. I love it, too! But in my house, we gravitate towards the simple po' boy buns that you can get from the grocery store. We butter them up and toast them on a griddle until golden, and they make for an amazing po' boy.

POT ROAST & GRAVY

MAKES ABOUT 4 SERVINGS

1   (2- to 3-pound) chuck roast
Pi-YAHHHHH!! Seasoning, to taste
All-purpose flour, for dusting
2   tablespoons vegetable oil
1   yellow onion, chopped
1   (8-ounce) package sliced fresh
     mushrooms
1   (2-ounce) package onion soup mix
1   cup water
2   tablespoons Worcestershire sauce
2   tablespoons Pickapeppa Sauce
1   tablespoon minced garlic
4   stalks celery, cut into 2- to 3-inch pieces
5   carrots, peeled and cut into 2- to 3-inch
     pieces
¼   cup cold water
2   tablespoons cornstarch
Mashed potatoes or hot cooked rice, to serve

1. Generously season both sides of roast with Pi-YAHHHHH!! Seasoning. Pat down seasoning on all sides. Dust the roast with flour on all sides.

2. In a large Dutch oven over a medium heat, pour oil. Add roast, and sear each side for 6 to 8 minutes. Monitor at the 5- to 6-minute mark in case the pot is too hot. Once the roast has a nice sear on each side, remove it from the pot, and place in a large bowl; set aside.

3. Add the onion to pot, and stir to break up drippings. Sauté for about 5 minutes; add mushrooms, and sauté for 20 minutes more.

4. Meanwhile, in a medium bowl, mix onion soup mix, 1 cup water, Worcestershire sauce, and Pickapeppa Sauce.

5. Add minced garlic to pot, and sauté for 5 minutes more. Add a small amount of soup mixture; stir. Push onion and mushroom mixture to one side, and add roast to the other side. Scoop some onion and mushroom mixture on top of roast. Pour remaining soup mixture over roast. Bring to a boil, cover, and lower heat to a simmer. Let cook for 1 hour.

6. Add the celery and carrots to the pot, pushing down along the sides. Bring to a slight boil. Cover, lower heat to a simmer, and cook for another 1½ hours. Remove roast from pot, place in a large bowl, and set aside.

7. In a small bowl, whisk together ¼ cup cold water and cornstarch. Slowly stir into the pot.

8. Cut roast into chunks, and return to pot. Cover and cook for 30 minutes more.

9. Serve over rice or mashed potatoes. Enjoy!

PORK ROAST & GRAVY

MAKES ABOUT 4 SERVINGS

1 (3- to 4-pound) boneless pork shoulder roast
Pi-YAHHHHH!! Seasoning, to taste
2 tablespoons vegetable oil
1 yellow onion, chopped
Cold water, as needed
1 (8-ounce) package sliced fresh mushrooms
1 tablespoon minced garlic
1 (14.5-ounce) can chicken broth
1 (2-ounce) package onion soup mix
2 tablespoons Worcestershire sauce
1 pound baby Dutch yellow potatoes, halved
6 carrots, peeled and cut into 2- to 3-inch pieces
¼ cup cold water
2 tablespoons cornstarch
Hot cooked rice or mashed potatoes, to serve
Garnish: fresh chopped parsley

1. Generously season both sides of the roast with Pi-YAHHHHH Seasoning. Pat down seasoning on all sides.

2. In a large pot over a medium-high heat, heat oil. Add roast, and sear for 6 to 8 minutes on each side. Monitor closely in case the pot is too hot. Once the roast has a nice sear on all sides, remove it from the pot, and place in a large bowl; set aside.

3. Add the onion to the pot, and stir, breaking up any drippings. If you have drippings that are really stuck to the bottom of the pot, just add a small amount of cold water. Sauté for about 5 minutes; add mushrooms, and sauté for 20 minutes more. Add garlic, and sauté for 5 minutes more.

4. Meanwhile, in a medium bowl, whisk together chicken broth, onion soup mix, and Worcestershire.

5. Add a small amount of the broth mixture to the sautéed vegetables. Stir, breaking up anything stuck to the bottom. Push vegetables to one side, and add roast to the other side. Scoop some sautéed vegetables on top of the roast. Pour remaining broth mixture over roast, and bring to a boil. Cover, reduce heat to a simmer, and let cook for 1 hour.

6. Add potatoes and carrots to the pot. Bring to a boil. Cover, reduce heat to a simmer, and let cook for 1½ hours more. Remove the roast from the pot, placing in a large bowl, and set aside.

7. In a small bowl, whisk together ¼ cup cold water and cornstarch. Slowly stir mixture into pot.

8. Cut roast into chunks, and return to pot. Cover and cook over a low heat for 30 minutes. Serve over rice or mashed potatoes. Garnish with fresh chopped parsley, if desired, and enjoy!

HAMBURGER STEAK & ONION GRAVY

MAKES 6 SERVINGS

Hamburgers:
2   pounds ground beef
½   cup Italian-seasoned bread crumbs
1   large egg
1   tablespoon Worcestershire sauce
½   tablespoon salt
1   teaspoon garlic powder
½   teaspoon ground black pepper
1   tablespoon vegetable oil

Gravy:
1   yellow onion, sliced
½   stick unsalted butter
¼   cup all-purpose flour
1   (14.5-ounce) can beef broth
1   cup water
1   teaspoon Pi-YAHHHHH!! Seasoning
1   teaspoon garlic powder

Mashed potatoes and corn, to serve
Garnish: fresh parsley leaves

1. For the hamburgers: In a large bowl, combine ground beef, bread crumbs, egg, Worcestershire, salt, garlic powder, and pepper. Divide mixture into 6 even portions, and shape each portion into a 5-inch patty.

2. In a large skillet, heat oil over a medium-high heat. Add 3 patties, and sear for 3 to 4 minutes on each side. Repeat with remaining patties. When done, place patties on a plate, and set aside.

3. For gravy: Add onion to the skillet. Stir onion to break up any cooked bits on the bottom of the skillet. After a few minutes, move onions to one side of skillet, and place butter on the opposite side. When butter has melted, add flour, and stir to combine. Sauté for about 20 minutes. Add a small amount of beef broth, and stir to combine. When mixture reaches a creamy consistency, add remaining beef broth. Add 1 cup water, Pi-YAHHHHH!! Seasoning, and garlic powder. Stir until combined, and bring to a slight boil. Cover, reduce heat to a simmer, and cook for 30 minutes.

4. Return hamburgers to skillet. Scoop some of the gravy over the patties. Increase heat, and bring to a slight boil. Cover, reduce heat to a simmer, and cook for 30 to 40 minutes more. Serve with mashed potatoes and corn. Garnish with parsley, if desired, and enjoy!

This is a group of the future generation, along with parents who care. Together, we work hard to not just create great martial artists but also outstanding individuals who care for their community

PI-YAHHHHH!! PATTY MELT

MAKES 1

½ stick salted butter, divided, plus more for toast
4 tablespoons vegetable oil, divided
1 yellow onion, chopped
¼ pound ground beef
Pi-YAHHHHH!! Seasoning, to taste
2 slices Texas toast
Pepper Mayo (recipe follows)
1 slice American cheese
1 slice Monterey Jack cheese with peppers

1. In a medium skillet, melt 2 tablespoons butter with 2 tablespoons oil over a low heat. Add onion; raise heat to medium, and cook, stirring occasionally, until browned, 8 to 10 minutes. Remove from skillet, and keep warm. Return skillet to a low heat. (If you have a griddle, heat one side to a high heat, and heat the other side to a low heat.)

2. Meanwhile, in another medium skillet, heat remaining 2 tablespoons oil over a high heat.

3. Shape beef into a 5-inch patty. Season one side generously with Pi-YAHHHHH!! Seasoning. Place patty, seasoned side down, in skillet with oil. Press with spatula to create an even sear. Cook for roughly 3 to 4 minutes or until sides of patty begin to brown.

4. Meanwhile, butter one side of each slice of Texas toast. Place one slice of toast, buttered side down, in skillet over low heat. Raise heat to medium. On other slice of toast, spread Pepper Mayo on the side without butter; set aside.

5. Spread Pepper Mayo on side of the toast facing up in the skillet, and place American cheese on top. Next, add some sautéed onions on top of American cheese.

6. After about 3 to 4 minutes, or when you start to see browning form on the side of the patty, turn it over. Let sear for another 3 minutes.

7. Remove patty from the high heat, and place on top of the onions and cheese on Texas Toast. Add a slice of Monterey Jack atop patty, and the other slice of Texas Toast, buttered side up. Carefully turn entire sandwich so you can sear the top piece of toast. Sear for about 5 to 6 minutes or until golden brown. Remove sandwich from heat, and enjoy!

Pepper Mayo

MAKES ABOUT ¾ CUP

½ cup mayonnaise
½ tablespoon yellow mustard
½ teaspoon garlic powder
½ teaspoon ground black pepper
½ teaspoon Worcestershire sauce

1. Combine all ingredients; set aside.

BLACK BELT TIP
You'll have some Pepper Mayo left over from this. Store it in your fridge and pull it out to make more patty melts, or just spread it onto any burger or sandwich. It'll add a punch of flavor.

This was the day when Pi-YAHHHHH!! Seasoning was officially in more than 100 stores in Louisiana.

OVEN-BAKED BABY BACK RIBS

MAKES 4 SERVINGS

2 tablespoons firmly packed light brown sugar
1½ tablespoons Pi-YAHHHHH!! Seasoning
½ tablespoon smoked paprika
1 rack baby back ribs
Barbecue sauce

1. Thoroughly mix together the light brown sugar, Pi-YAHHHHH!! Seasoning, and smoked paprika in a small bowl. Set aside.

2. Remove the rack of ribs from the package it came in, and place on a layer of paper towels. Pat down the ribs on both sides with paper towels. There is a thin layer of membrane on the bottom side of the ribs. You want to pinch and pull one end of this membrane and slowly peel it off. It will almost look like some kind of thin see-through paper. Once you have the membrane removed, pat down once again with paper towels.

3. Begin evenly sprinkling all sides of the ribs with the sugar mixture. Gently pat down the seasoning on each side.

4. Once you have all sides of the ribs seasoned, place the ribs on a large baking sheet layered with foil; cover with foil. It's good to put the ribs in the refrigerator for at least 1 hour or even overnight to let the seasoning settle.

5. When you are getting close to cooking time, preheat your oven to 275°.

6. Bake, covered, for 4 hours. Increase the oven temperature to 325°, and remove the foil from the top of the ribs. Bake for another 15 minutes. (It's OK if reaching the 325° mark takes up 5 of those minutes.) Take two pairs of tongs, gently grab a good portion of each end of the rack of ribs, and turn over. Coat the bottom side with two coats of your favorite barbecue sauce. Turn the ribs back over, and apply two coats to the top of the ribs with your favorite barbecue sauce. Bake for another 5 minutes. Let stand for about 5 minutes. Slice the ribs according to your desired thickness, serve, and enjoy!

BLACK BELT TIP

What I love about these ribs is that they're pretty hands-off. You don't have to fire up a smoker or grill and monitor them all day. I like to prep and season the ribs the night before and then throw them in the oven the next morning. By lunch, they're ready. Make my Baked Bean Casserole on page 223 and some Potato Salad on page 232 to go with it and you're ready to go!

STICKY CHICKEN

MAKES 8 SERVINGS

4 to 5 pounds bone-in skin-on chicken
    (thighs and drumsticks)
Pi-YAHHHHH!! Seasoning, to taste
2   teaspoons garlic powder
2   tablespoons all-purpose flour
1   stick salted butter
4   yellow onions, chopped (about 6 cups)
2   cups chicken stock
¼   cup cold water (optional)
2   tablespoons cornstarch (optional)
Hot cooked rice, to serve
Garnish: fresh parsley

1. Coat all sides of the chicken with generous amounts of Pi-YAHHHHH!! Seasoning and the garlic powder. Dust each side of the chicken with the flour.

2. In a large pot over a low heat, add the butter. As butter melts, raise the heat to medium-high. When the butter begins to bubble, add the chicken, layering pieces tightly next to one another. Brown chicken for 6 to 8 minutes on each side. (Could possibly be less, depending on how high your heat is.) Place chicken in a large bowl, and set aside.

3. Add onions to the pot. Stir, breaking up any remaining drippings on bottom of pot. Sauté for 25 to 30 minutes.

4. Add a small amount of chicken stock to the pot. Stir, breaking up any browning that may be stuck to bottom of pot. Return chicken to the pot. Pour in any liquid that may be left in the bowl the cooked chicken was in. Add remaining chicken stock. Bring to a boil. Cover, lower heat to a simmer, and let cook for 2 hours. It's OK to stir every 20 minutes or so.

5. At the end of 2 hours, if you want to thicken the gravy, you can mix ¼ cup cold water and cornstarch, and blend in. Serve with some rice, garnish with parsley, if desired, and enjoy!

These are Misty's parents.
We often take leftovers to their house.
They don't live too far from us and
are always welcoming to leftovers.
Gotta share the love!

CHICKEN SAUCE PIQUANT

MAKES 8 TO 10 SERVINGS

4 to 5 pounds chicken thighs, legs, and wings
2   teaspoons garlic salt
2   teaspoons black pepper
1½   cups all-purpose flour, divided
1   stick butter
⅔   cup vegetable oil
1   yellow onion, chopped
1   green bell pepper, chopped
2   stalks celery, chopped
1   (6-ounce) can tomato paste
1   (14.5-ounce) can fire-roasted diced
     tomatoes
1   (10-ounce) can mild diced tomatoes with
     green chiles
1   tablespoon minced garlic
1   (32-ounce) container chicken broth
2   (15-ounce) cans tomato sauce
2   cups water
2   tablespoons granulated sugar
1   tablespoon Pi-YAHHHHH!! Seasoning
1   tablespoon dried parsley
Hot cooked rice, to serve
Garnish: dried parsley flakes

1. Season chicken with garlic salt and black pepper. Dust chicken with ½ cup flour to coat. Shake off excess.

2. In a large skillet over a medium heat, melt butter. Raise heat to medium-high. In batches, add chicken, and sear for 6 to 8 minutes on each side. (May be less, depending on how high the heat is.) Remove the chicken as you see both sides brown up nicely.

3. While chicken is searing, get started on the roux. In a large pot over a low heat, add oil and remaining 1 cup flour. Begin stirring immediately. Consistently stir until you reach a brown caramellike color. During this process, make sure you keep an eye on the chicken. Try to manage time between the pot and pan evenly to prevent anything from burning.

4. When all pieces of chicken have browned up evenly, move chicken to a large bowl.

5. Add onion, pepper, and celery to skillet over a medium-low heat. Stir vegetables, loosening any remaining drippings left over from chicken. Meanwhile, continue to stir roux. Sauté vegetables for 10 minutes. Add tomato paste, and sauté for 10 minutes more. Add the fire-roasted diced tomatoes, diced tomatoes with green chiles, and minced garlic. Cook for 10 minutes more. If roux still hasn't reached a caramel color, cover the pan of vegetables, reduce heat to a simmer, and come back to it every so often as you continue to cook the roux.

6. Once roux reaches a caramel color, slowly add in a small amount of chicken broth. Stir until you reach a creamy mixture.

7. Add remaining chicken broth to tomato-vegetable mixture. Pour the tomato mixture in with the roux, and blend evenly. Add the tomato sauce, 2 cups water, sugar, Pi-YAHHHHH!! Seasoning, and parsley. Mix well. Add chicken to pot, and push each piece down into the sauce. Pour in any remaining juices from the bowl the cooked chicken was in. Increase heat, and bring to a slight boil. Cover, lower heat to a simmer, and cook for 2 hours, stirring the bottom every 15 minutes. Serve with rice, garnish with parsley flakes, if desired, and enjoy!

CARROTS AND GROUND MEAT

MAKES 8 SERVINGS

1 tablespoon vegetable oil
2 pounds ground beef
½ stick salted butter
2 yellow onions, chopped
1 pound carrots, peeled and sliced
1 (32-ounce) container chicken stock
1 tablespoon Pi-YAHHHHH!! Seasoning
1 teaspoon garlic powder
2 cups long-grain rice
Garnish: chopped fresh parsley

1. Start out by heating a large pan or pot over a medium heat.

2. Add the oil to the pan. Add the beef. Cook, gently moving the beef around, until browned and crumbly. You can let it sit at times. Remove the beef from the pan, and place in a bowl on the side.

3. Reduce the heat to low. Wipe down the pan so no small bits are left in the pan. Add the butter to the pan. Once the butter has melted, add the onions. Sauté the onions for 15 minutes.

4. Add the carrots to the pan, and sauté for another 15 minutes. Add a small amount of chicken stock, and break up anything stuck to the bottom. Add the rest of the chicken stock. Add the Pi-YAHHHHH!! Seasoning and garlic powder. Add the beef back to the pan. Bring the heat up to reach a boil. Once you've reached a boil, cover, lower to a simmer, and let it cook for 1 hour.

5. Add the rice to the pan. Bring the heat back up to a boil. Once you've reached a boil, cover, lower to a simmer, and cook for 25 minutes.

6. Turn the heat off, remove the pan from the heat, and let sit, covered, for another 5 minutes. Sprinkle with parsley, if desired. Serve and enjoy!

Christian Fulgium is a former professional mixed martial artist out of Louisiana. He currently does restoration work for homes and businesses. He was a huge help getting my house back in order after my patio caught fire one spring.

It wouldn't be Thanksgiving in the Derouen household without fried turkey.

7 | REAL DEAL SEAFOOD MEALS

SUPPERS FROM THE GULF

SHRIMP AND SAUSAGE JAMBALAYA

MAKES 6 TO 8 SERVINGS

2 pounds peeled and deveined medium fresh shrimp
½ tablespoon Pi-YAHHHHH!! Seasoning
1 tablespoon vegetable oil
1 pound smoked pork sausage, sliced into whole and half-moon slices
1 yellow onion, chopped
1 green bell pepper, chopped
2 stalks celery, chopped
1 bunch green onions, chopped
3 cloves garlic, chopped
1 (32-ounce) container chicken stock
2½ cups long-grain rice
1 tablespoon hot sauce
1 tablespoon browning and seasoning sauce
1 teaspoon salt
Garnish: chopped fresh parsley, hot sauce

1. Start out by heating an oven-safe pot over a medium heat. Also, preheat your oven to 300°.

2. Sprinkle the shrimp with the Pi-YAHHHHH!! Seasoning. Blend evenly, and refrigerate.

3. Add the oil to the pot. Add the sausage to the pot. Sear the sausage for about 10 minutes or until a thin brown layer has formed across the bottom of the pot. Be careful not to burn. Remove the sausage, and drop in the yellow onion, bell pepper, celery, and green onion. Stir until you get up all the drippings from the bottom. Sauté for about 10 minutes. Add the garlic. Sauté for another 15 minutes.

4. Add a small amount of the chicken stock to the pot, and blend. Add the sausage back to the pot. Add the rest of the chicken stock. Add the rice, hot sauce, browning and seasoning sauce, and salt, and blend. Raise the heat, and bring to a slight boil. Once you've reached a boil, add in the shrimp. Stir, and bring back to a slight boil; cover.

5. Bake for 1 hour. Let stand, covered, for another 5 minutes. Uncover, and stir. Garnish with parsley and hot sauce, if desired, and enjoy!

In May of 2020, I received a YouTube Silver Play Button for surpassing 100,000 subscribers. This meant a lot to me. I wouldn't be here without all of the great people who make my recipes and support me.

CATFISH COURTBOUILLON

MAKES 8 TO 10 SERVINGS

2 sticks salted butter
1 yellow onion, chopped
2 stalks celery, chopped
1 green bell pepper, chopped
1 red bell pepper, chopped
1 bunch green onions, chopped
4 cloves garlic, chopped
2 tablespoons all-purpose flour
1 (6-ounce) can tomato paste
2 (15-ounce) cans tomato sauce
1 (28-ounce) can crushed tomatoes
1 (10-ounce) can diced tomatoes with green chiles
1 tablespoon granulated sugar
1 tablespoon dried parsley
½ tablespoon salt
½ tablespoon ground black pepper
2 dried bay leaves
¼ teaspoon cayenne pepper (optional)
2 cups hot water
2 to 3 pounds catfish fillets
Pi-YAHHHHH!! Seasoning, to taste
Hot cooked rice, to serve
Garnish: chopped green onion

1. Start out by heating a large pot over a medium-low heat.

2. Melt the butter in the pot. Once the butter has melted, add in the yellow onion, celery, bell peppers, green onion, and garlic. Sauté for 40 minutes.

3. Move the vegetables to one side of the pot, and add the flour to the opposite side. Blend the flour in. Continue to cook down for 10 more minutes. Add the tomato paste. Cook for another 10 minutes. Add the tomato sauce, crushed tomatoes, diced tomatoes, sugar, parsley, salt, black pepper, bay leaves, and cayenne (if using). Mix well. Add the 2 cups hot water. Bring to a slight boil; cover, lower to a simmer, and let cook for 1 hour.

4. While the sauce is cooking, season both sides of your catfish fillets with Pi-YAHHHHH!! Seasoning. Keep cool until ready.

5. When the 1 hour is up on the sauce, add your catfish fillets to the sauce, pushing each fillet under the sauce. Raise the heat back up to a slight boil; cover, lower to a simmer, and cook for 1 hour. Serve with rice; garnish with green onion, if desired, and enjoy!

Bringing home the bacon!
Or, in this case, the fish.

SHRIMP CREOLE

MAKES 6 TO 8 SERVINGS

8   cups water
2   pounds medium fresh shrimp
2   yellow onions
2   stalks celery
1   bunch green onions
1   dried bay leaf
1   green bell pepper
1   red bell pepper
4   cloves garlic
2   sticks salted butter
⅓   cup all-purpose flour
1   (10-ounce) can diced tomatoes with green chiles
1   (28-ounce) can crushed tomatoes
1   tablespoon granulated sugar
1   tablespoon dried parsley
1   tablespoon Pi-YAHHHHH!! Seasoning
1   teaspoon salt, divided
¼   teaspoon cayenne pepper
2   cups long-grain rice

1. Start out by heating a large pot over a low heat. Also, heat a pot filled with 8 cups water over a low heat.

2. Peel and devein the shrimp. If you have peelings, save them for your stock. Put the shrimp in the refrigerator for now.

3. Cut off the ends of the yellow onions, tops and bottoms of the celery, and tops and bottoms of the green onions. Add the cut pieces of vegetables, shrimp peelings, and bay leaf to the pot of water. If you do not have shrimp peelings, do not worry; just proceed without. Raise the heat so the pot reaches a boil. Once you've reached a boil, cover and lower to a simmer. Simmer for 1 hour.

4. Meanwhile, chop the bell peppers, garlic, remaining yellow onion, remaining celery, and remaining green onion.

5. Melt the butter in the large pot. Increase your heat to a medium heat. Add the chopped vegetables to the pot, and simmer for 30 minutes.

6. Push as much of the vegetables to one side as you can, and add the flour to the opposite side. Blend until smooth, and mix with the vegetables. Sauté for 20 minutes, stirring continuously.

7. Strain the stock through a fine-mesh sieve into a large bowl. Let sit until needed.

8. Add the diced tomatoes to the vegetable mixture. Sauté for another 5 minutes. Add the crushed tomatoes and 2 cups of the shrimp stock. Add the sugar, parsley, Pi-YAHHHHH!! Seasoning, ½ teaspoon salt, and cayenne. Blend evenly. Raise the heat to bring the sauce to a slight boil. Once you see some slight bubbling, cover the pot, and lower to a simmer. Cook for 1 hour and 20 minutes, stirring every 5 minutes to break up anything sticking to the bottom.

9. After about 45 minutes of cooking, you want to get started cooking some rice. Use the rice, 4 cups of the leftover stock, and remaining ½ teaspoon salt. Bring to a boil; cover, lower to a simmer, and let it cook for 25 minutes. Remove the pot from heat, and let sit for another 5 minutes before uncovering.

10. With about 20 minutes left of cooking the sauce, be sure to remove the shrimp from the refrigerator. After the sauce has simmered for the allotted time, add the shrimp to the sauce. Stir, cover, and let simmer for another 10 to 15 minutes. Serve over rice, and enjoy!

SHRIMP AND GRITS

MAKES 10 TO 12 SERVINGS

Sauce:
1   pound smoked sausage
1   stick salted butter, divided
½   yellow onion, chopped
1   stalk celery, chopped
Top half 1 bunch green onions (save some green onion for garnish), chopped
2   cloves garlic, chopped
¼   cup all-purpose flour
4   cups Homemade Shrimp Stock (recipe on page 38)

Grits (see Black Belt Tip):
4   cups Homemade Shrimp Stock (recipe on page 38)
4   cups whole milk
2   cups grits
2   cups (8 ounces) shredded Cheddar cheese
½   stick salted butter
2   teaspoons salt
1   teaspoon ground black pepper

3 to 4 pounds medium fresh shrimp, peeled and deveined (tails left on 8 to 12 for garnish)
2   tablespoons salted butter
Pi-YAHHHHH!! Seasoning, to taste

1. For sauce: Cut up two-thirds of your sausage into quarter pieces and the rest into half-moon pieces. Set aside.

2. Heat a sauté pan over a medium to medium-low heat. Once heated, add ½ stick butter. After the butter has melted, drop in the sausage, and lightly sear. Remove the sausage, and place on a plate to the side.

3. Next, drop in your yellow onion, celery, green onion, and garlic, stirring frequently to deglaze the bottom of the pan. Once you've gotten everything up from the bottom of the pan, drop in the flour. Be careful with your heat at this point. After blending in the flour, drop in remaining ½ stick butter. Stir consistently until you see a light caramel-looking color. (This could take 30 minutes or more.)

4. Add your sausage and half of your Shrimp Stock to the pan. Once you've blended that in, add the remaining Shrimp Stock. Bring to a slight boil; cover, lower to a simmer, and cook for 1 hour.

5. For grits: When there's about 20 to 30 minutes left on your sauce, you want to get started making your grits. To a large pot, add Homemade Shrimp Stock and milk, and bring to a boil over a medium-high heat. When the liquid begins to boil, slowly whisk in grits, and lower heat to medium-low. Cook until grits are soft and creamy, about 15 minutes. Stir in cheese, butter, salt, and pepper. Cover and keep warm until you're ready to serve.

6. When the hour is up on your sauce, add in your fully peeled shrimp. Cook, uncovered, for 20 minutes.

7. At this time, you can heat a small sauté pan over a medium heat. Add the butter.

8. Meanwhile, season your shrimp with the tails on with Pi-YAHHHHH!! Seasoning. Drop them into your sauté pan, and cook for about 2 minutes on each side.

9. After your sauce has been cooking for 20 minutes, you're good to go. Plate with some grits, some shrimp sauce, a few of your garnish shrimp, and some garnish green onions. Enjoy!

BLACK BELT TIP

The amounts of ingredients for the grits and the cook times will vary based on the grits you use. Follow the package directions to compare. Use shrimp stock and milk for any liquid needed, and be sure to add butter, black pepper, and cheese to flavor to your liking.

FRIED CRAB CAKES

MAKES 6

½   stick salted butter
1   yellow onion, chopped
1   green bell pepper, chopped
2   stalks celery, chopped
3   cloves garlic, chopped
1   bunch green onions, chopped
⅓   cup chopped fresh parsley
2   large egg yolks
1   pound lump crabmeat, picked free of shell
¼   cup seasoned bread crumbs
¼   cup mayonnaise
½   lemon, juiced
1   tablespoon Dijon mustard
½   tablespoon Pi-YAHHHHH!! Seasoning
½   tablespoon Worcestershire sauce
½   tablespoon hot sauce
2   cups vegetable oil
2   large eggs
Panko (Japanese bread crumbs)
Rémoulade sauce, to serve

1. Start out by heating a large pan over a medium to medium-low heat.

2. Melt the butter in the pan. Add the yellow onion, bell pepper, celery, and garlic, and sauté for 10 minutes.

3. Add the green onion and parsley to the pan. Sauté for another 10 minutes or until all vegetables are very tender. Once vegetables are very tender, remove from pan, and place in a bowl.

4. In a large bowl, whisk the egg yolks. Add the sautéed vegetables, crabmeat, seasoned bread crumbs, mayonnaise, lemon juice, mustard, Pi-YAHHHHH!! Seasoning, Worcestershire, and hot sauce. Gently fold mixture using clean hands. Shape into patties. With this amount, you should be able to make 6 crab cakes around the size of a hamburger bun. After you've made all your crab cakes, cover them, and freeze for 1 to 2 hours.

5. Begin heating oil in a large pan over a medium to medium-high heat.

6. In a small shallow bowl, whisk the eggs; in a shallow dish, place panko. Dip crab cakes, one at a time, into the eggs and then coat with the panko.

7. Carefully drop crab cakes, one at a time, into the oil. When you begin to see the sides turn a golden color, that's when they're ready to turn. Once both sides are golden, remove from oil, and set on a plate layered with paper towels. Let cool for a few minutes. Serve with rémoulade sauce, and enjoy!

BLACK BELT TIP

Make sure you use some kind of tool that helps compact the crab cakes. I use a biscuit cutter. This also helps keep each of the crab cakes the same size.

CRAWFISH BURRITO CASSEROLE

MAKES 8 SERVINGS

1½ sticks salted butter, divided
1 yellow onion, chopped
1 green bell pepper, chopped
2 stalks celery, chopped
⅓ cup all-purpose flour
1 tablespoon minced garlic
1 (10-ounce) can diced tomatoes with green chiles
½ tablespoon granulated sugar
1 quart heavy whipping cream
1 tablespoon Pi-YAHHHHH!! Seasoning
½ tablespoon chili powder
2 pounds Louisiana crawfish tails
1 (16-ounce) block Velveeta Jalapeño or Velveeta Queso Blanco
10 to 20 large flour tortillas, cut into square and rectangle shapes
Garnish: sliced fresh jalapeño and cilantro leaves

1. Start by heating a large pot and a large pan over a medium heat.

2. Drop ½ stick butter into your pan. Once the butter has melted, add in your onion, bell pepper, and celery, and let them cook down for about 15 minutes, stirring occasionally.

3. At this point, preheat your oven to 350°.

4. Once you've got your vegetables cooking, get a roux started in your large pot. Add your remaining 1 stick butter, and let melt. Add in your flour, and stir constantly until you get a peanut butter color. This can be tricky because you want to stir your vegetables occasionally as well. Adjust your heat accordingly so as not to burn. If you get to a peanut butter color quickly, just turn the heat off and let it sit. It will be fine.

5. Add the garlic to the vegetable mixture, and sauté for 10 minutes. Add the tomatoes and sugar. Let it cook down for 5 minutes. Add the heavy cream. Add the Pi-YAHHHHH!! Seasoning and chili powder. Mix well.

6. If you have a peanut butter color roux, add the contents of the pan to the roux, and mix well. Add the crawfish, and let cook for 10 minutes.

7. Cut half of the Velveeta into slices, and add to the pot. Freeze the other half of the Velveeta.

8. Once the mixture is creamy throughout, you want to begin putting together the casserole. Spray the bottom of a 13x9-inch baking dish with cooking spray.

9. Layer the bottom of the dish with about one-third of the tortilla pieces. Spread a few spoonfuls of the creamy crawfish mixture over the tortillas. Then add another layer of tortillas. Repeat 1 to 2 more times depending on how much you've spread or how deep the dish is. The top layer should be the creamy crawfish mixture. Grate the other half of your Velveeta, and sprinkle across the top.

10. Bake for 20 minutes. Let cool for 5 to 10 minutes. Garnish with jalapeño and cilantro, if desired. Serve, and enjoy!

Louisiana crawfish can´t be beat.

CRAWFISH ÉTOUFFÉE

MAKES ABOUT 6 SERVINGS

2	sticks salted butter
2	yellow onions, chopped
2	stalks celery, chopped
1	green bell pepper, chopped
1	red bell pepper, chopped
1	bunch green onions, chopped
1	tablespoon Pi-YAHHHHH!! Seasoning
¼	teaspoon salt
¼	teaspoon cayenne pepper
4	cloves garlic, chopped
⅓	cup all-purpose flour
2	cups hot water (add more if desired)
2	pounds Louisiana crawfish tails

Hot cooked rice, to serve
Garnish: chopped green onion

1. Start out by heating a pot or large pan over a low heat.

2. Drop butter into your hot pot, and melt completely. Raise the heat to medium, and add the yellow onion, celery, bell peppers, most of the green onion, Pi-YAHHHHH!! Seasoning, salt, and cayenne, and cook for about 20 minutes.

3. Add the garlic to the vegetable mixture, and cook, stirring occasionally, for another 10 minutes. Push the vegetables to one side of the pot; add the flour, and blend into the butter. Once the flour is mixed in well, stir everything together, and cook until you start to see the mixture turn brown, 30 to 40 minutes. Be very cautious of the flour burning during this time. If the heat seems a little high, lower it.

4. With about 3 minutes left of cooking, add a little bit of the hot water to the pot, and stir until it's a creamy mixture. Add the crawfish and the rest of the hot water to the pot. Blend evenly. Raise the heat to where you see a slight boil. Cover and lower to a simmer. Cook for 15 to 20 minutes.

5. If you feel as though you would like a thinner sauce, just add a little more water. Taste to see if you need more seasoning. Serve with rice, and garnish with some chopped green onion, if desired. Enjoy dat!

This is my daughter Zoey's absolute favorite.

TALES FROM THE BAYOU

This hands down might be my favorite southern Louisiana dish. There is genuinely nothing like it. There is such a depth of flavor from the buttery base and all the vegetables cook down in it. I've never eaten anything else in my life and said, "That tastes like étouffée." I've only eaten étouffée and said, "That's a dang good étouffée." I always remember being so excited when my mom said she was making it. It's amazing now to see the same reactions in my kids' eyes. My little Zoey lights up when Daddy says, "I'm making crawfish étouffée today."

SHRIMP ÉTOUFFÉE

MAKES 6 TO 8 SERVINGS

2   sticks salted butter
2   yellow onions, chopped
2   stalks celery, chopped
1   green bell pepper, chopped
1   red bell pepper, chopped
1   bunch green onions, chopped
6   cloves garlic, chopped
1   tablespoon Pi-YAHHHHH!! Seasoning
¼   teaspoon seasoning salt
¼   teaspoon cayenne pepper
⅓   cup all-purpose flour
2   cups hot water (add more if desired)
2   pounds peeled and deveined small fresh shrimp

1. Start out by heating a large pot or pan over a low heat.

2. Drop the butter into your pot, and melt completely. Add the yellow onion, celery, bell peppers, green onion, and garlic, and raise the heat to a medium heat. Add the Pi-YAHHHHH!! Seasoning, seasoning salt, and cayenne. Sauté for about 30 minutes.

3. Push the vegetables to one side of the pot; add the flour to the opposite side, and blend into the butter. Once the flour is mixed in well, stir everything together. Sauté for another 30 to 40 minutes or until the flour becomes brown in color. Be very cautious during this time. If the heat seems a little high, lower it. You don't want anything to burn to the bottom.

4. With about 3 minutes left of cooking, add a little bit of the hot water to the pot, and stir, breaking up anything on the bottom, until it's a creamy mixture. Add the rest of the hot water to the pot. Raise the heat to where you see a slight boil. Cover and lower to a simmer. Cook for 30 minutes, stirring every 5 to 10 minutes and breaking up anything trying to stick to the bottom.

5. Add the shrimp to the pot, and let simmer for another 10 to 15 minutes. If you feel as though you would like a thinner gravy, just add a little more water. However, also taste it to see if you need more seasoning. Enjoy!

Taekwondo has always been my first love, but it has been an absolute honor to train Jiu-Jitsu with the team over at Next Generation Martial Arts. The respect and camaraderie for one another has far exceeded my expectations. My understanding of what it means to be a white belt became so clear when I started training here. Every amazing work of art starts with a blank canvas. It takes time and work to make it art. When I had my very first white belt, I didn't understand that. Since becoming a black belt in Taekwondo and then beginning again as a white belt in a different martial art, it all makes sense to me now.

I dedicate a big part of my life to Taekwondo, and I wouldn't change that for anything.

8 | *SIDEKICKS*
SOUTHERN VEGGIES AND CASSEROLES

SMOTHERED CABBAGE

MAKES 6 SERVINGS

1   tablespoon vegetable oil
1   pound smoked tasso, cut into chunks
1   yellow onion, chopped
1   medium head cabbage
1   tablespoon minced garlic
1   (14.5-ounce) can chicken broth
1   tablespoon Pi-YAHHHHH!! Seasoning
2   tablespoons cold water
1   tablespoon cornstarch
Hot cooked rice (optional), to serve

1. Start out by heating a large pot over a medium heat.

2. Add the oil to the hot pot, and drop in the tasso. Sear the tasso for about 5 minutes; remove from the pot.

3. Add the onion to the pot, and sauté for 20 minutes.

4. Meanwhile, take time to prep the cabbage by cutting into quarters. Remove and discard the center stem from each quarter of cabbage. Chop the cabbage into large pieces.

5. Add the minced garlic to the onion. Sauté for another 5 minutes. Add a small amount of the chicken broth. Stir and break up any bits stuck to the bottom. Add the rest of the broth. Add the tasso and Pi-YAHHHHH!! Seasoning. Give it a good stir. Add the cabbage. Gently fold the bottom to the top so that much of the cabbage can touch the broth. Raise the heat to high to reach a slight boil.

6. Once you see or hear a slight boil under the cabbage, cover the pot, lower to a simmer, and cook for 50 minutes, stirring the bottom cabbage to the top every 10 minutes so all the cabbage can cook evenly. Uncover, and raise the heat to medium; cook for another 10 minutes.

7. In a small bowl, stir together the 2 tablespoons cold water and cornstarch.

8. Push the cabbage to one side of the pot, and gradually mix in the cornstarch slurry. This will help the juices in the pot thicken into a gravy. From here, serve over rice (if using) or eat plain. Enjoy!

TALES FROM THE BAYOU

Instructing children is challenging but so rewarding. I hold martial arts in such a high regard. It is truly amazing what it can do for a person, especially when the person starts at a young age. There are so many life lessons along the way that help build confidence, perseverance, humility, honor, integrity, and so much more. To watch a child blossom into an outstanding adult, and know that you were part of that, is something money cannot buy. It's an honor to have been a student, but it is a blessing to be an instructor.

DIRTY RICE

MAKES 8 TO 10 SERVINGS

1 tablespoon vegetable oil
1 pound ground chuck
1 pound hot blend breakfast sausage
1 teaspoon salt
½ stick salted butter
1 yellow onion, chopped
1 green bell pepper, chopped
2 stalks celery, chopped
1 bunch green onions, chopped
1 tablespoon minced garlic
2 beef bouillon cubes
1 (32-ounce) container chicken stock
3½ cups water
1 tablespoon Pi-YAHHHHH!! Seasoning
1 tablespoon browning and seasoning sauce
4 cups long-grain rice

1. Start out by heating a large oven-safe pot over a medium-low heat.

2. Add the oil to the pot. Drop the beef and sausage in. Blend the meat together, and add the salt. Once all the meat has become browned and crumbly, remove the meat with a slotted spoon, and place in a bowl on the side.

3. At this time, preheat your oven to 300°.

4. Drop the butter into the pot. Once the butter has melted, add the yellow onion, bell pepper, celery, and green onion. Cook down for 25 minutes. Add the garlic and beef bouillon cubes. Cook for another 5 minutes. Add the meat back to the pot. Add the chicken stock. After you've blended in the stock, add the 3½ cups water, Pi-YAHHHHH!! Seasoning, and browning and seasoning sauce. Raise the heat to high so you can reach a boil. At this time, add the rice, and mix well. Once you've reached a boil, cover, turn the heat off, and place the pot in the oven.

5. Bake for 1 hour. Let sit for 5 minutes before uncovering it. Uncover, stir, serve, and enjoy!

BLACK BELT TIP

Some also like to add ground chicken liver and gizzards to their dirty rice. It's up to you.

BLACK-EYED PEAS

MAKES 6 TO 8 SERVINGS

1 (16-ounce) package dried black-eyed peas
½ stick salted butter
1 pound smoked tasso, cubed
1 yellow onion, chopped
1 green bell pepper, chopped
2 stalks celery, chopped
1 tablespoon minced garlic
1 (32-ounce) container chicken broth
1 tablespoon Pi-YAHHHHH!! Seasoning
½ teaspoon garlic salt
½ teaspoon ground black pepper
1 dried bay leaf
Cornbread, to serve

1. Start out by heating a pot over a low heat. Also, at this time, get a separate pot of water boiling.

2. Wash the black-eyed peas in a sieve, and set aside.

3. Melt the butter in the hot pot. As you see the butter melting, raise the heat to a medium. Add the tasso, and let sear for about 5 minutes. Remove tasso, and place in a separate bowl.

4. Add the onion, bell pepper, and celery to the pot. Sauté for 25 minutes.

5. Meanwhile, your water should have begun boiling. Add the peas to the water, and boil, uncovered, for 10 minutes. Strain the peas through a sieve over a separate pot or bowl, reserving the water. Let this sit until you're done sautéing your vegetables.

6. Add the minced garlic to your vegetables, and sauté for another 5 minutes. Add the tasso, chicken broth, and 2 cups of the reserved water. Add the Pi-YAHHHHH!! Seasoning, garlic salt, black pepper, and bay leaf. Blend well, and bring to a boil. Once you've brought it to a boil, cover and lower to a simmer. Keep covered and cook for 2 hours.

7. Cook the peas to your desired consistency. You may need to add more water. Discard bay leaf. Serve with cornbread, and enjoy!

This is Dustin Poirier, a famous Louisiana mixed martial artist. He's one of my top all-time favorite fighters. Throughout this book, you'll often see his hot sauce, Poirier's Louisiana Style Hot Sauce.

LIMA BEANS

MAKES 6 TO 8 SERVINGS

1 (16-ounce) package dried large lima
 beans
½ stick salted butter
1 pound smoked tasso, cut into chunks
1 yellow onion, chopped
1 green bell pepper, chopped
2 stalks celery, chopped
1 tablespoon minced garlic
1 (32-ounce) container chicken broth
1 tablespoon Pi-YAHHHHH!! Seasoning
½ teaspoon garlic salt
½ teaspoon ground black pepper
1 dried bay leaf
Hot cooked rice, to serve
Garnish: chopped fresh parsley

1. Start out by heating a medium pot of water over a high heat.

2. After you turn the heat on, wash your lima beans and then drop them into the pot of water. Let it come to a boil. Once you see the beans come to a boil, set a timer for 10 minutes. Leave uncovered. Be cautious of your heat so it doesn't boil over.

3. In a separate pot, melt the butter over a low heat. Once the butter has melted, add the tasso, and sear for about 5 minutes. Remove the tasso, and place in a bowl.

4. Add the onion, bell pepper, and celery to the hot pot. Begin stirring occasionally over the next 10 minutes over a medium heat. Add the tasso back in, and let cook 10 minutes more.

5. When the 10-minute timer is up for the beans, drain through a sieve over a bow to reserve the bean broth.

6. When the 20 minutes is up on sautéing the vegetables and tasso, add the minced garlic. Sauté for another 5 minutes. Add a small amount of chicken broth to break up the bottom drippings. Once you've gotten all the drippings up from the bottom of the pot, add in the rest of the chicken broth, lima beans, and 2 cups of the reserved bean broth. Add the Pi-YAHHHHH!! Seasoning, garlic salt, black pepper, and bay leaf. Raise the heat to bring to a boil. Once it has reached a boil, cover the pot, lower to a simmer, and let cook for 2 hours.

7. After the beans have cooked down, discard the bay leaf. If you want thicker beans, remove about 1 cup of beans with a slotted spoon and put into a bowl on the side. Mash the beans to a creamy consistency and then add back to the pot. Do this until you find your desired consistency. Serve over rice. Garnish with parsely, if desired, and enjoy!

SEAFOOD CORNBREAD STUFFING

MAKES 8 TO 10 SERVINGS

½ stick salted butter
1 yellow onion, chopped
1 green bell pepper, chopped
1 red bell pepper, chopped
1 stalk celery, chopped
1 bunch green onions, chopped
1 tablespoon minced garlic
1¼ cups water
½ pound chopped peeled and deveined fresh shrimp
½ pound lump crabmeat, picked free of shell
1 (10.5-ounce) can cream of mushroom soup
1 teaspoon Pi-YAHHHHH!! Seasoning
1 (8- to 12-ounce) package cornbread mix, baked according to package directions, cooled, and crumbled
1 (8-ounce) block Monterey Jack cheese with peppers, shredded

1. Heat up a large pot over a low heat.

2. Add your butter to the pot, and let melt. As you see the butter melting, raise the heat to medium. Add your yellow onion, bell peppers, celery, and green onion, and cook, stirring occasionally, for about 20 minutes.

3. Add the garlic to your vegetables, and cook down for another 5 minutes.

4. Preheat your oven to 350°.

5. Add the 1¼ cups water to the vegetables, and stir. Break up anything stuck to the bottom. Add the shrimp, crabmeat, soup, and Pi-YAHHHHH!! Seasoning, and stir. Add the cornbread and cheese; mix well.

6. Spray a 13x9-inch baking dish with cooking spray. Pour the mixture into the dish.

7. Bake for 35 to 40 minutes. Let cool for 5 to 10 minutes, and serve.

Cornbread stuffing is a Thanksgiving necessity in my book, and I put my Cajun touch on it by adding fresh lump crabmeat and shrimp to the mix.

CRAWFISH CORNBREAD DRESSING

MAKES 10 TO 12 SERVINGS

½ stick salted butter
1 yellow onion, chopped
1 green bell pepper, chopped
1 red bell pepper, chopped
1 stalk celery, chopped
1 bunch green onions, chopped
1 tablespoon minced garlic
1½ cups water
1 (10.5-ounce) can cream of mushroom soup
½ tablespoon Pi-YAHHHHH!! Seasoning
1 (7- to 8-ounce) block jalapeño Havarti cheese, cubed
1 (12-ounce) package cornbread mix, baked according to package directions, cooled, and crumbled
1 pound crawfish tails

1. Heat up a large pot over a low heat.

2. Add the butter to the pot, and let melt. Add the yellow onion, bell peppers, celery, and green onion, and cook, stirring occasionally, for about 25 minutes.

3. Preheat your oven to 350°.

4. Add the garlic to the vegetable mixture, and sauté for about 5 minutes more. Add the 1½ cups water, and stir. Add the soup and Pi-YAHHHHH!! Seasoning, and stir. Add your cubed cheese, and mix until melted. Fold in the cornbread. Turn off the heat, and mix in the crawfish.

5. Butter and spray a 13x9-inch baking dish. Pour the mixture into the dish.

6. Bake for 35 to 40 minutes. Let cool for 5 to 10 minutes, and then serve.

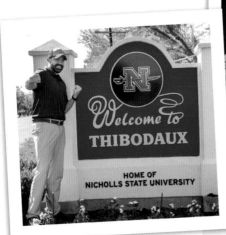

I was raised in Houma, Louisiana, but I was born right here in Thibodaux. After spending a few years in Broussard, Louisiana, my wife and I decided to plant our feet back in Thibodaux. Most people do not know this, but every cooking video I have ever done was right here in Thibodaux. I love this town. It's family-oriented and very supportive of its locals. They even gave me the key to the city. Although, I can say with certainty that it still doesn't unlock Chick-fil-A on Sunday. LOL.

BAKED BEAN CASSEROLE

MAKES 10 SERVINGS

1   **pound thick-cut bacon**
1   **Vidalia onion, chopped**
1   **red bell pepper, chopped**
1   **pound ground beef**
1   **tablespoon minced garlic**
½   **tablespoon Pi-YAHHHHH!! Seasoning**
4   **(15-ounce) cans pork and beans in tomato sauce**
½   **cup dark molasses**
¼   **cup firmly packed light brown sugar**
¼   **cup barbecue sauce**
2   **tablespoons yellow mustard**

1. Start out by heating a large pan over a medium heat.

2. Sear the bacon in the large pan to almost crispy; remove to a plate layered with paper towels. Be sure to leave the drippings in the pan.

3. Add the onion and bell pepper to the pan, and sauté for 25 minutes.

4. While the vegetables are sautéing, chop the bacon.

5. Add the beef, garlic, and Pi-YAHHHHH!! Seasoning to the vegetable mixture. Cook until the beef is browned and crumbly. Drain in a sieve over paper towels, and add back to pan. Discard the paper towels. Add in the bacon, pork and beans, molasses, brown sugar, barbecue sauce, and mustard. Mix well. Cover and lower to a simmer. Let simmer for 30 minutes, stirring occasionally.

6. At this time, preheat your oven to 350°.

7. Pour the contents of the pan into a 13x9-inch baking dish.

8. Bake for 50 minutes. Let cool for 5 to 10 minutes before serving. Enjoy!

TALES FROM THE BAYOU

Louisiana is the only state that has the letters "USA" running right through the middle. I decided to start selling shirts that showcased this. Misty and I wore ours to celebrate the Fourth of July. I enjoy the Fourth of July for many reasons, first and foremost, just to celebrate our freedoms. I understand that many people debate about many things, but one thing holds true: we are allotted many freedoms in this country. If you ever want to compare, just do some research on other countries. I'm blessed to live right here with my fellow Americans. Another reason is the food. It's always been a great tradition to light the pit on the Fourth of July. However, in my humble opinion, you can't have great barbecue without great side dishes. This Baked Bean Casserole is simply amazing. It's everything I love about baked BBQ beans with ground beef thrown in the mix. Add this one to your list next time you throw it down. Trussme.

WHITE BEANS & HAM

MAKES 8 SERVINGS

1 pound dried white navy beans
½ stick unsalted butter
1 pound smoked diced ham
½ pound smoked tasso, chopped
1 yellow onion, chopped
1 green bell pepper, chopped
2 stalks celery, chopped
7 cups water, divided
1 (32-ounce) container chicken broth
3 cloves garlic, minced
1 tablespoon Pi-YAHHHHH!! Seasoning
1 tablespoon dried parsley
1 teaspoon salt
2 dried bay leaves
Hot cooked rice, to serve
Garnish: chopped fresh parsley

1. Start out by washing the beans and setting them off to the side.

2. Heat a large pan over a medium heat.

3. Add half of the butter to the pan. Once the butter has melted, add in the ham and tasso. Sauté the ham and tasso until you start to see some browning form on the bottom of the pan. Remove the meat from the pan, and add the remaining butter. Add in the onion, bell pepper, and celery. Sauté for roughly 25 minutes.

4. Meanwhile, in a separate pot, add the beans, 5 cups water, and chicken broth. Bring to a boil. The moment you've reached a hard boil, boil, uncovered, for 10 minutes. Watch the heat to be careful that the liquid doesn't boil over.

5. Back in the pan, once your vegetables have sautéed for the allotted time, add the garlic, and sauté for another 5 minutes. Add a small amount of the remaining 2 cups water. Stir the bottom of the pan so you break up any remaining bits on the bottom. Add the meat and rest of the 2 cups water to the pan. Stir.

6. Once the 10 minutes is up on the beans, add the vegetable mixture to the pot of beans. Add the Pi-YAHHHHH!! Seasoning, dried parsley, salt, and bay leaves. Stir well.

7. Bring to a boil, cover, lower to a simmer, and let simmer for 3 to 4 hours. After 3 hours, check the texture of the beans. If they still seem hard, keep simmering. When the texture is to your liking, you can thicken the consistency by gently mashing beans on the side of the pot and stirring. Do this until you get the desired consistency. Simmering some more uncovered will also thicken them. Serve with rice, sprinkle with parsley, if desired, and enjoy!

BLACK BELT TIP

Many beans recipes tell you to soak the dry beans beforehand, but with this recipe, there's no need. They cook long and slow, and they get nice and soft. Serve with cornbread and you can make a whole meal out of these beans.

BAKED MACARONI & CHEESE

MAKES 12 SERVINGS

2 teaspoons salt, divided
1 (16-ounce) package large elbow macaroni
2 sticks salted butter
½ cup all-purpose flour
1 quart heavy whipping cream, room temperature
1 teaspoon ground black pepper
1 (16-ounce) block medium Cheddar cheese, shredded and divided
1 (8-ounce) block Colby-Jack cheese blend, shredded
2 (12-ounce) cans evaporated milk
4 large egg yolks
Paprika, to taste

1. Heat a large pot of water over a high heat. As the water is reaching a boil, add 1 teaspoon salt to the water. Boil the pasta for the lowest time on the package directions; drain, and let cool.

2. Preheat the oven to 350°.

3. In another large pot, melt butter over a low heat. Once the butter is completely melted, add the flour, and begin stirring. You want to keep stirring until you reach a peanut butter color. Once the roux has reached a peanut butter color, gradually stir in half of the cream. When the first half has blended evenly, go ahead and add the rest. Add the pepper and remaining 1 teaspoon salt. Add half of the Cheddar and all the Colby-Jack. Stir until cheese has completely melted.

4. In a small bowl, combine evaporated milk and egg yolks. Mix well. Add a few tablespoons of cheese sauce and stir to combine. Add the mixture back into the cheese sauce. Gently mix in the macaroni. If the pasta has clumped together, don't worry; just keep moving it around in there and it will break up.

5. Spray a 13x9-inch baking dish with cooking spray. Add the macaroni and cheese to the pan. Sprinkle the remaining Cheddar over the top. At this time, you can also sprinkle some paprika for a nice look.

6. Bake for 30 minutes. Let cool for about 10 minutes before serving. Enjoy!

BLACK BELT TIP

In step 4, you'll notice I tell you to temper the eggs. If you were to drop the egg yolks directly into the hot cheese sauce, you'd run the risk of scrambling them. So, to avoid that, we mix the yolks with the evaporated milk and a little bit of the warm cheese sauce so the whole mixture becomes nice and smooth when you add everything back together. Don't skip this step.

JALAPEÑO MAC & CHEESE

MAKES 12 SERVINGS

2 sticks salted butter
3 jalapeños, seeds removed and chopped
1 yellow onion, chopped
2 tablespoons Pi-YAHHHHH!! Seasoning
1 tablespoon minced garlic
1 quart heavy whipping cream
1 (14.5-ounce) can chicken broth
2 (12-ounce) packages elbow macaroni
1 (16-ounce) block Velveeta Jalapeño or Velveeta Queso Blanco, cubed
1 (8-ounce) block Monterey Jack cheese with peppers, shredded

1. Start out by heating a large pot over a very low heat. Heat another large pot filled with water over a medium-high heat.

2. Add the butter to the pot over a low heat. Once the butter is halfway melted, raise the heat to a medium heat. Add the jalapeños and onion, and sauté for 20 minutes. Add the Pi-YAHHHHH!! Seasoning and garlic. Sauté for another 5 minutes. Add the cream and chicken broth, and lower the heat to a low setting.

3. Preheat the oven to 350°.

4. Around this time, start cooking the macaroni according to the package directions.

5. Add the Velveeta to the pot with the sauce. Gradually stir until melted.

6. When the macaroni is done, drain, and add it to the cheese sauce. Shut the heat off, and gently stir in the macaroni until sauce begins to thicken.

7. Spray a 13x9-inch baking dish with cooking spray, and pour the macaroni into the dish. Top with the Monterey Jack.

8. Bake, uncovered, for 25 to 30 minutes. Let stand for 5 to 10 minutes, and enjoy!

BLACK BELT TIP

This mac & cheese is very creamy and has the perfect kick. Don't be scared of the spice. Between the Pi-YAHHHHH!! Seasoning, the jalapeños, and the spicy cheese, you may think the heat will be overwhelming, but it's not. Trussme. I've even been known to throw some of this mac & cheese on a chili dog. Do dat! You won't regret it.

CORN MAQUE CHOUX

MAKES 8 TO 10 SERVINGS

3 (12-ounce) bags frozen corn kernels
1 yellow onion
1 red bell pepper
2 jalapeños
1 stick salted butter
1 tablespoon minced garlic
1 tablespoon Pi-YAHHHHH!! Seasoning
½ pint heavy whipping cream

1. Pour the frozen corn in a 5-quart pot; add enough water to cover by about 1 inch. Bring to a boil over a high heat. As soon as you see the water boiling, turn the heat off, and drain. Rinse thoroughly with cold water so the corn stops cooking. Set aside for now.

2. Heat a medium pot over a low heat.

3. Chop the onion and bell pepper. Slice the jalapeños in half; carve out the inside, and chop. (For a spicy Corn Maque Choux, chop up 1 jalapeño without carving out the inside.)

4. Add the butter to the hot pot. As you see the butter begin to melt, raise the heat to a medium heat. Drop in your chopped vegetables, and sauté for 20 minutes.

5. Add the garlic and Pi-YAHHHHH!! Seasoning to the pot. Sauté for another 5 minutes. Add the corn, and gradually stir in the cream. Cover and lower to a simmer. Cook for another 5 minutes. Serve, and enjoy!

TALES FROM THE BAYOU

If you've watched my videos, you know that my family loves corn. We eat it as a side with tons of dishes. So, when my followers started commenting to ask me to make Corn Maque Choux, I knew I had to do it. Corn Maque Choux is a Creole dish that is popular here in Louisiana. During the summer, when corn is in season, it's the perfect side for any meal. But, frozen corn works just as well, and using frozen means you can eat it any time of year. When I first made this recipe, my daughter Zoey lit up. She loved it so much, she ate bowls and bowls. She was even eating it as her after-school snack!

POTATO SALAD

MAKES 6 CUPS

3 pounds Yukon gold potatoes, peeled and cut into quarters
1 tablespoon salt
3 large in-shell eggs
1 tablespoon minced garlic
2 tablespoons water
1 cup mayonnaise
2 tablespoons yellow mustard
1 tablespoon Pi-YAHHHHH!! Seasoning

1. Start out by heating a large pot of water over a high heat.

2. When the water begins boiling, add the potatoes and salt. Boil for 20 minutes.

3. In a separate pot, add the eggs and enough water to cover by 1 inch. Turn the heat to a high setting. As soon as you see the water boiling, boil for 2 minutes. Turn the heat off, and let them stand in the hot water for 15 minutes. You will want to have a bowl of ice water on the side. Remove the eggs, and put them in the ice water for roughly 5 minutes.

4. Peel the eggs, cut in half, gently remove yolks, and set to the side. Chop the whites of the eggs, and set aside.

5. When the potatoes are done, drain through a colander, and place them in a large bowl. Slightly mash the potatoes.

6. In a small microwave-safe container, add the garlic, and heat in the microwave for roughly 20 seconds. Add the yolks and 2 tablespoons water to the garlic, and mix well.

7. To the bowl of potatoes, add the garlic mixture, egg whites, mayonnaise, mustard, and Pi-YAHHHHH!! Seasoning. Mix well, and you're ready to serve.

TALES FROM THE BAYOU

I think everybody does potato salad differently. Some add pickles, some throw in hard-boiled eggs, some drop in more mustard and mayo than others. No two people make it alike, and that's alright! I always say make it how you like it. Cajun potato salad, though, is traditionally a little chunky and a little creamy. I like the potatoes to be slightly mashed so that it has a smoother consistency. If ya know, ya kneaux! Potato salad is one of those dishes that serves multiple roles in Cajun cuisine. It can be served as a side at picnics and barbecues, of course, but true Cajuns know it's best eaten in a big bowl of crawfish stew. It may sound weird if you've never tried it, but something about the creamy consistency of the potato salad with the warm stew is outta this world. Some folks even put it in their gumbo. Like I always say, you deux you!

My girls love helping me make king cake every Mardi Gras.

9 | *DEROUEN FAMILY DESSERTS*
SWEETS FOR EVERY SEASON

CHOCOLATE CHIP COOKIES

MAGES 24

2½ cups enriched self-rising flour
¾ cup firmly packed light brown sugar
¼ cup granulated sugar
1 teaspoon baking soda
¼ teaspoon salt
3 tablespoons canola oil
1 large egg
2 sticks unsalted butter, melted and cooled slightly
⅔ cup semisweet chocolate chips

1. Preheat the oven to 375°.

2. In the bowl of a stand mixer fitted with the paddle attachment, mix the flour, sugars, baking soda, and salt on a low setting. Make sure these ingredients thoroughly mix together so the brown sugar has broken up completely. Turn the mixer off when mixed well.

3. Add the oil and egg to the flour mixture. Turn the mixer back on a low setting. Gradually pour in the melted butter. Let the mixer blend all ingredients for a few minutes. Gradually pour in the chocolate chips. (Do not overmix.) Once all the chocolate chips are blended in, turn the mixer off.

4. Scoop dough by about 1 tablespoon, and place roughly 2 inches apart on an ungreased baking sheet. Feel free to press in a few chocolate chips on the top of each scoop for visible chocolate chips.

5. Bake on the top rack for 10 to 12 minutes. Let cool for 10 minutes, and enjoy!

The little ninjas especially love these cookies.

CHOCOLATE CHIP BANANA PUDDING

MAKES 12 SERVINGS

1   (14-ounce) can sweetened condensed milk
1   (8-ounce) block cream cheese, softened
1   (5.1-ounce) package vanilla instant pudding mix
2½ cups whole milk
1   (16-ounce) container frozen whipped topping, thawed
1   (16-ounce) package chocolate chip cookies
1   (11-ounce) package vanilla wafers
4   ripe bananas, sliced

1. In the bowl of a stand mixer fitted with the paddle attachment, beat the condensed milk, cream cheese, and pudding mix at a medium speed until creamy. Once you've reached a creamy mixture, keep beating, and gradually add the milk. Keep mixing until you reach a pudding-like consistency, about 5 minutes. You may have to stop the mixer and scrape the bottom a few times. Once you've reached a pudding-like consistency, add the whipped topping, and fold it in gently. Set the mixture aside when complete.

2. In a 13x9-inch baking dish, layer some chocolate chip cookies and vanilla wafers. Spread half of the banana slices out sporadically over the cookies and wafers. Pour half of the pudding mixture over the top of the bananas. Spread evenly. Repeat the cookie/wafer, banana, and pudding mixture layers again. For the final layer, spread out some wafers; crush up your remaining chocolate chip cookies, and sprinkle across the top. Cover and refrigerate for at least 1 hour. Enjoy!

This is my li'l Juliet and our dog Hazel the day we got her. We love Hazel. She's a part of the family, but we like to call her HazelNUT because, let me tell you, that dog is very much a nut.

CHOCOLATE PEANUT BUTTER PIE

MAKES 2 (9-INCH) PIES

2 (8-ounce) blocks cream cheese, softened
2 cups creamy peanut butter
1½ cups granulated sugar
½ tablespoon vanilla extract
2 (8-ounce) containers frozen whipped topping, thawed and divided
2 (9-inch) chocolate piecrusts
1 (11.75-ounce) jar hot fudge, warmed
¾ cup chocolate chips

1. In the bowl of a stand mixer fitted with the paddle attachment, beat cream cheese, peanut butter, sugar, and vanilla extract together until you have a creamy consistency, about 5 minutes. Use a rubber spatula to fold in 1 container of whipped topping into the creamy mixture.

2. Split the creamy peanut butter mixture between the piecrusts. Freeze for 1 hour.

3. Pour a desired even amount of hot fudge over each pie, using the whole jar between the two pies. Spread the remaining container of frozen whipped topping over both pies. Sprinkle each pie with chocolate chips. Enjoy!

BLACK BELT TIP

I use the chocolate piecrusts that you can find in the baking section of your grocery store. This pie makes 2, so it's a great dessert if you're feeding a crowd. Otherwise, make one for yourself and give another to a friend, or just eat both yourself. You deux you.

I couldn't do this without the support of my family. This is my little niece Jolene when she spied Uncle Jason on some Pi-YAHHHHH!! Seasoning in the grocery store.

BREAD PUDDING WITH RUM SAUCE

MAKES 8 SERVINGS

Bread Pudding:
1   **large loaf French bread**
1   **stick salted butter**
1½ **cups granulated sugar**
2   **teaspoons ground cinnamon**
¼   **teaspoon ground nutmeg**
6   **large eggs**
1   **quart heavy whipping cream**
1   **(14-ounce) can sweetened condensed milk**
1   **(12-ounce) can evaporated milk**
2   **teaspoons vanilla extract**

Rum Sauce:
½   **stick salted butter**
¼   **cup firmly packed light brown sugar**
½   **tablespoon vanilla extract**
¼   **cup dark rum**
¾   **cup whole milk, divided**
¼   **cup confectioners' sugar**
1   **tablespoon cornstarch**

Sweetened whipped cream and fresh strawberries, to serve

1. Start out by preheating your oven to 300°.

2. For bread pudding: Slice the bread into 1- to 2-inch cubes. Place the pieces of bread on a large baking sheet.

3. Bake for 30 minutes. When done, place the bread in a large bowl to let cool. Leave oven on.

4. Grease a 13x9-inch baking dish with the stick of butter, using only enough to grease the dish. Melt the remaining butter in a container, and let it cool.

5. In a bowl, whisk together the granulated sugar, cinnamon, and nutmeg.

6. In the bowl of a stand mixer fitted with the whisk attachment, beat the eggs on low speed for about 1 minute. Add the melted butter, cream, condensed milk, evaporated milk, and vanilla extract. Turn the mixer to a low setting; sprinkle in the sugar mixture.

Allow the ingredients to mix for about 1 minute. Pour the mixture over the bread in the bowl.

7. Place a lengthy loose sheet of cling wrap over the bread mixture. Take a bowl that is just a tad smaller than the bowl the bread is in, fill it with a small amount of water, and place it on top of the bread mixture. Gradually add more water so that the top bowl presses down on the bread, allowing all the bread to submerge in the liquid. Be cautious as you do this. If the top bowl is too heavy, liquid will spill out of the bottom bowl. Let this sit for 30 minutes. About midway through, remove the cling wrap and gently fold the bottom bread to the top. Place another layer of cling wrap over the bread, and place the bowl of water back on top.

8. Pour the bread mixture into the baking dish. Gently press down the bread so that some of the remaining liquid surfaces. Cover with foil.

9. Bake for 1½ hours. Remove the foil, and bake for an additional 30 minutes. Let cool for 20 to 30 minutes.

10. Meanwhile, for rum sauce: Heat a small pan over a low heat. Add the butter. When the butter has melted, raise the heat to a medium heat. Add the brown sugar and vanilla extract. Blend evenly. Once you have a smooth mixture, stir in the rum. Let cook for a couple of minutes, allowing the alcohol to cook out. Add ½ cup milk and confectioners' sugar. Mix well.

11. In a small bowl, stir the cornstarch and the remaining ¼ cup milk. Add the mixture to the sauce by pouring and stirring at the same time. Raise the heat slightly, and keep stirring. When you see the sauce start to thicken, turn the heat off. Stir constantly for a few more minutes. Pour the sauce over the bread pudding, and serve with whipped cream and strawberries. Enjoy!

KING CAKE

MAKES 1 TO 2 CAKES (SEE BLACK BELT TIP)

Dough (for 2 cakes):
1   stick salted butter
1   (8-ounce) block cream cheese
½   cup lukewarm water
½   cup plus 1 tablespoon granulated sugar, divided
2   (0.25-ounce) packages active dry yeast
½   tablespoon salt
1   cup whole milk
2   large eggs
6   cups all-purpose flour

Filling (for 1 cake):
⅓   cup granulated sugar
⅓   cup firmly packed light brown sugar
1½   tablespoons ground cinnamon
1   stick salted butter, divided

Topping (for 1 cake):
2   cups confectioners' sugar
1 to 2 tablespoons whole milk
Purple, gold, and green sanding sugars

1. For dough: Start out by heating a small pot over a low heat. Melt the butter and cream cheese in the pot.

2. In a small bowl, combine the ½ cup lukewarm water, 1 tablespoon granulated sugar, and yeast. Let sit for at least 10 minutes.

3. Add the salt and remaining ½ cup granulated sugar to the melted butter mixture. Once you have a creamy consistency, add the milk, stir, and turn the heat off. Add the mixture to the bowl of a stand mixer, and let cool down.

4. Once the mixture has cooled down, add the yeast mixture and eggs. Attach a dough kneader to mixer, and turn mixer on a low setting. Add the flour to the bowl, and mix for 5 to 6 minutes. (If you do not have a dough kneader attachment, mix by hand, kneading the dough until the smooth look has formed.)

5. Spray some cooking spray in a large bowl. Place the dough in that bowl; cover with a damp towel, and let sit for 2 hours.

6. For filling: In a small bowl, blend the sugars and cinnamon. Set aside.

7. Punch out the dough a couple times, and cut into equal halves.

8. Place one half of the dough on a large floured surface. Flip on both sides so that all sides of dough are floured.

9. Melt half of the butter in the microwave for about 30 seconds.

10. Roll the dough into a rectangle shape measuring out to about 2½x1½ feet. Begin spreading the melted butter on the flattened dough. Spread the sugar mixture all over the top of the flattened dough. Roll the dough into the form of a jelly roll.

11. Layer a pan with parchment paper, and spray with cooking spray. Gently place the roll on the parchment paper. Tuck the bottoms, and connect the ends. Pinch the dough all the way around so that ends are fully connected. Cover with a damp towel, and let sit for 40 minutes.

12. At this time, preheat your oven to 350°.

13. Melt the remaining butter in the microwave for roughly 30 seconds. Spread the melted butter over the dough.

14. Bake for 30 to 40 minutes, depending on the calibration of your oven. Just be on the lookout for a light golden color. Let cool for 20 to 30 minutes.

15. Meanwhile, for topping: In a medium bowl, mix together the confectioners' sugar and milk to a thick, pouring consistency.

16. Add the icing and sanding sugar to the king cake in sections. Spread sugar in sections of purple, gold, and green. Cut a slice, and enjoy!

BLACK BELT TIP

This recipe makes enough dough for two king cakes, but if you plan to make two, be sure to double the filling and the topping ingredients. If you're only making one, you can vacuum seal the other half of the dough and place in the freezer for later.

APPLE COBBLER

MAKES 6 TO 8 SERVINGS

Filling:
7 to 8 Honeycrisp apples (about 3 pounds)
¼ cup cold water
3 tablespoons cornstarch
1 cup firmly packed light brown sugar
½ lemon, juiced
2 tablespoons salted butter
½ tablespoon ground cinnamon

Crust:
2½ cups all-purpose flour
½ cup granulated sugar
1 tablespoon baking powder
1 stick salted butter, melted
1 cup whole milk
1 large egg

Topping:
1 tablespoon granulated sugar
1 tablespoon firmly packed light brown sugar
½ teaspoon ground cinnamon

Ice cream, to serve

1. Preheat oven to 350°.

2. For filling: Peel and thinly slice the apples, removing the cores. Set them in a 13x9-inch baking dish.

3. In a small bowl, mix the ¼ cup cold water and cornstarch.

4. To a small pot, add the cornstarch slurry, brown sugar, lemon juice, butter, and cinnamon. Heat over a low heat. Once the butter is almost fully melted, turn the heat off, and let sit for a couple minutes. Pour the mixture over the apples, and gently stir around so that every apple has been covered with the mixture. Let sit for now.

5. For crust: In the bowl of a stand mixer fitted with the paddle attachment, add the flour, granulated sugar, and baking powder. Turn the mixer to a low setting. After the dry ingredients mix for a couple minutes, add the melted butter, milk, and egg. Mix until all ingredients are blended and you have a doughy consistency.

6. Scoop the dough out over the apples, spreading as evenly as you can. It is OK if you have some holes in some areas. The dough will expand in the oven.

7. For topping: Mix the sugars and cinnamon. Sprinkle evenly over the dough.

8. Bake until the top is golden and the filling is bubbly, about 40 to 50 minutes. Let cool for 5 to 10 minutes before serving. Serve with ice cream. Enjoy!

BLACK BELT TIP

This apple cobbler is a great dessert for holiday meals. It's pretty simple to make, and everyone loves it, especially with a big scoop of vanilla ice cream over top.

PECAN PRALINES

MAKES ABOUT 20

1   **cup plus 2 tablespoons heavy whipping cream, divided**
1   **cup granulated sugar**
1   **cup firmly packed light brown sugar**
½   **stick salted butter, melted**
1   **cup chopped pecans**
¼   **teaspoon vanilla extract**

1. Start out by heating a 5-quart pot over a medium-high heat.

2. Stir in 1 cup cream, sugars, and melted butter. Let the mixture come to a boil, stirring constantly. You're going to see a lot of bubbling. Just keep stirring constantly, moving things around. A flat-end wooden spoon or spatula is helpful here. Keep stirring for roughly 10 minutes. Right at about the 10-minute mark, the mixture will start to darken a bit. The mixture will even appear to be drying up a bit, almost getting crumbly. This is when you will turn the heat off, and stir in the pecans, vanilla, and remaining 2 tablespoons cream. The added cream will help bring the mixture back to a creamy consistency.

3. Once you reach the creamy consistency, let the mixture sit for about 1 minute. Scoop tablespoonfuls of mixture (or your desired serving size) onto a sheet of parchment paper. Let the pralines cool for about 1 hour before eating. Enjoy!

I don't know where I'd be without these ladies. Often people ask, "Aren't you going to try for a boy?" and I'll respond, "Don't you think I did!" LOL. To be quite honest, I couldn't imagine life without them, and I never feel like anything in my life is missing.

RECIPE INDEX

RESOURCES:
Find The Cajun Ninja on Facebook at *facebook.com/thecajunninja*, on YouTube at *youtube.com/thecajunninja*, and on Instagram and TikTok at @thecajunninja.

Pi-YAHHHHH!! Seasoning is available at Rouses Markets, H-E-B, Mac's Fresh Market, and various other retailers. It is available online at *thecajunninja.com*.

All personal photography was provided by Jason Derouen.

EDITORIAL

**Chairman of the Board/
Chief Executive Officer**
Phyllis Hoffman DePiano

President/Chief Creative Officer
Brian Hart Hoffman

VP/Culinary & Custom Content
Brooke Michael Bell

Group Creative Director
Deanna Rippy Gardner

Art Directors Ann McKeand Carothers,
Timothy H. Robinson

Senior Project Editor Anna Hartzog

Senior Culinary Editor Georgia Clarke

Copy Editor Meg Lundberg

Test Kitchen Director Laura Crandall

Food Stylists Kathleen Kanen, Kellie
Gerber Kelley, Vanessa Rocchio

Stylists Lily Simpson, Dorothy Walton

Creative Director/Photography
Mac Jamieson

Photographers Jim Bathie, Steve Rizzo

COVER
Photography by Jim Bathie
Food Styling by Vanessa Rocchio
Styling by Dorothy Walton

PRODUCTION & MARKETING

President/Chief Operating Officer
Eric Hoffman

EVP/Operations and Manufacturing
Greg Baugh

VP/Digital Media Jon Adamson

Marketing Director Kristy Harrison